D1491869

FIRST AWAKENINGS

The Early Poems of Laura Riding

LAURA RIDING

First Awakenings:
THE EARLY POEMS

**Edited by Elizabeth Friedmann,
Alan J. Clark and Robert Nye**

CARCANET

First published in Great Britain in 1992 by
Carcanet Press Limited
208-212 Corn Exchange Buildings
Manchester M4 3BQ

A CIP catalogue record for this book is
available from the British Library.
ISBN 0 85635 985 8

The publisher acknowledges financial assistance
from the Arts Council of Great Britain

Set in 10pt Palatino by Bryan Williamson, Darwen
Printed and bound in England by SRP Ltd, Exeter

Contents

Editors' Introduction

This book consists of early poems by Laura Riding, all of them dating from the years 1920-1926, none of them published in her *Collected Poems* of 1938 nor in any of the nine separate volumes on which that collection draws. Most of the poems come from a cache of work mainly in typescript form which, its author later noted, "represents what I rejected for inclusion in my first book of poems – the manuscript of which, prepared for delivery to the English publisher, I took with me on my departure [for England] in December 1925." These poems, left in the safekeeping of a friend in America, were rediscovered only in 1979; they are now in the Berg Collection of the New York Public Library. To them the editors of the present volume have added a separate sequence of poems published in magazines – under the poet's first authorial name, Laura Riding Gottschalk – in the period 1922-26, but similarly uncollected in any of her books. Poems from the work now in the Berg Collection which had seen magazine appearance have been relocated in this final section because here it has been possible to establish a chronology at least of publication. With the Berg poems there is no such chronology, and the poems are printed in the four groups in which they were found. The first three of these sequences had their poems arranged by title in roughly alphabetical order; we have made that order word-by-word exact for all four.

In preparing this book we have sought to carry out Laura (Riding) Jackson's wishes, as expressed in the Preface. Her few unusual spellings have been retained where evidently intentional, as have the few instances of unorthodox punctuation; obvious errors have been silently corrected.* No poem is included here which was included in any of the books of poems she published in her lifetime; nor have we included any poem which was revised by her for such inclusion. A list of all omitted poems will be found in Appendix B.

The book therefore contains no line of verse which has previously appeared in any other book by Laura Riding, all of it falling

---

* The poem of Sequence IV, 'Can Lips Be Laid Aside?', originally appeared to the editors to be complete; we took the comma concluding our working typescript to be accidental, and altered it to a full-stop. At a late stage in preparation of the present volume, re-examination of this poem's original typescript showed evidence of intended continuation. We have decided to reinstate the final comma.

outside the canon of the *Collected Poems*. In terms of time, it covers the period from her beginnings as a poet while a student at Cornell to the publication of her first volume *The Close Chaplet* in the autumn of 1926. The title *First Awakenings: The Early Poems of Laura Riding* was given to the collection by the author herself in the last year of her life.

Acknowledgements

The poems in Sequences I-IV are reproduced by courtesy of the Henry W. and Albert A. Berg Collection, the New York Public Library, Astor, Lenox and Tilden Foundations. The poem in Appendix C, 'Address to Shelley', is by courtesy of the Jesse E. Wills Fugitive/Agrarian Collection, Vanderbilt University Library.

The editors gratefully acknowledge the assistance of Esther Antell (Mrs Joseph Henry Cohen); William Harmon of the University of North Carolina, Chapel Hill, and his former graduate assistants Susan Prahinski and Catherine Cowen; Francis O. Mattson and Stephen Crook of the Berg Collection, New York Public Library; and Marice Wolfe and Michael Sims, Special Collections, Vanderbilt University Library.

Author's Preface

My essential concern as to this material is that no use be made of it that would stimulate infusion of it into the published body of my poetic work – *Collected Poems*, 1938 and 1980, the self-determining canon of it. The *Collected Poems* text represents my text that I gathered into finality as the poetic work as known by me in its progressive consistency with itself in its, my, adherence to the possibilities of personal eloquence in the service of the great much standing just outside the door of human readiness to know what may be done, of the good to be done, waiting to be let in for saying. Any critical historicizing over poetic texts that I excluded from the collected representation of my progression in the path of the poetic possibilities of such eloquence, any analysis of what I excluded from it in the form of entire poems or portions of poems, with particularistic dwelling on revisions, verbally minor, incidental or quantitatively substantial, with intent of 'research' for historical tracing of my work's development, would be especially destructive of apprehension of the on-and-on sense-clarification of itself that the whole achieved, kept on achieving, until it reached a term in the kind of eloquence to the service of which I dedicated it (dedicated my personal powers of eloquence).

A historical analysis of the entire *archival* content of my production of poetic writing would materialize the essential sense and spirit of the work that *Collected Poems* comprehensively defines into a biographical synthesis, a collage formed of all the pieces and parts of my poetic work, converting it as it were into a quasi-autobiographical picture of it in a critico-biographical frame.

The mistakenness of a historicizing, an exegetical stock-taking of my poetic writing in its documentary bulk – which includes, besides the 'find' of what I left behind in my departing for abroad with the text of my first book of poems almost not fitting into the final space of what had to come with me, early poems published in magazines, either absent from *The Close Chaplet* or reproduced there with differences not represented in the 'find' in any form – would be both in its personal and in its critical implication. My poetic career was not a personal adventure, in the characteristic modern vein of psychological enterprise, or linguistically experimental in the characteristic modern vein of literary radicalism. The story of my poetic career was maliciously mutilated, as a personal and a critical story, in a book in which the critical readings of my work are personal readings, especially distorted for critical application, and the Truth I am depicted as 'pursuing' is represented as the object of an obsessive insistence on, and morbid striving for, certainty. The case for this reading of my poetic career, the temper of the thought-experience I put to the trial of poetic expression, was constructed by a tearing apart of the body of my poetic work into poem-pieces for particularistic interpretation. There was, here, ill-willed purpose not to see the work as a whole. Such piece-by-piece dissective treatment of it exposes the possibilities of distortion in the analytical singling-out of particulars for clues to general matters of significance. Not even good-willed purpose to see in the whole could be safe from going astray in the ramifications of exegetically thorough attention either to my *Collected Poems* as a body of poetic particularities, the mastering of them expected to be generally illuminating critically and personally, or to the additionally available archival poetic material, or to the composite bulk of both units of quantity arbitrarily construed as constituting my poetic work in the whole.

Laura (Riding) Jackson

I

A Bird Speaks

You think I am a pretty little bird, don't you,
Poised here on the tip of the roof,
A delicate silhouette for a limpid sky
Recklessly speckled with the fingerprints of the sunset.

A dainty picture.
Perhaps you will walk home thinking of me
And write a little poem:
>A pretty little bird
>Delicately poised
>Against the sky,
>Resting a moment
>On a roof-top
>At the end of the day,
>Thinking of his little ones
>In the nest swung high in the wood,
>Thinking of the wet wood
>Sweet with dew.

Just so.
You are human,
And hence sentimental (it's quite the same thing),
And have no sense of humor in consequence.
Else you would understand
Why I flee the wood
With its monotony of loveliness.
What! you say,
The green leaves,
And the blue sky,
And the pretty eggs in the nest?
I beg your pardon, Madam,
But I prefer a little dust pile on Catherine Street
To a green leaf:
It is not so well known.
The sky?
If you will believe me, Madam,
It is an inescapable bore.
If you had used it as much as I
You'd hardly blame me, I'm sure,
For hopping inquisitively in city streets

And watching people from window sills.
The eggs, the dear little eggs?
I think I have, perhaps, a dowdy mate
Drowsing over them somewhere....
But we'd never understand each other, Madam.

For instance, to-day:
I was in Brooklyn, Myrtle Avenue, they call it
(You could never feel the fascination of that name
And that street),
Myrtle Avenue, a web of fire-escapes
Indifferently unsentimental.

I like the back yards best,
With the steps of clotheslines
And the chorus of pulleys on Monday mornings.
You can never know the joy
Of perching blithely on a sill
To watch an old tin boiler trickle suds upon a stove
And a little half-dressed girl playing in the corner
On a heap of unwashed clothes.

New York is, of course, quite interesting,
Except for Central Park and the Drive.
Once I had the good fortune to peep into the Morgue.
Chinatown is charming, if you know it,
Not dangerous at all, but dirty....
But I'm sure we'd never understand each other, Madam.

Perhaps I will sing you a rapturous little song
On the sweetness of the Bowery.
It would be such fun
To see you thrill enchantedly,
Thinking what a nice carol I was singing
To the trees
And the green leaves
And the little eggs home on the nest.

A City Seems

A city seems between us. It is only love,
Love like a sorrow still
After a labor, after light.
The crowds are one.
Sleep is a single heart
Filling the old avenues we used to know
With miracles of dark and dread
We dare not go to meet
Save as our own dead stalking
Or as two dreams walking
One tread and terrible,
One cloak of longing in the cold,
Though we stand separate and wakeful
Measuring death in miles between us
Where a city seems and memories
Sleep like a populace.

A Dirge for Summer

My life is like the bitten tree, furzy and frazzled,
Neither a brave of elegance or accident.
How does the tree live, greened and bedazzled
Under a strange sun; dark with pride may the bark be,
But oh! the nibbled leaves hang full of shame and sorrow,
Float plaintively in the wind, unfree
Of flight. What can a tree say to a tree but this:
"Our life is like the sick soul of a man,
The stricken imperfection of a lost plan.
What is the good of beauty that escapes the flower,
Gleams like a sinister flash of fate, summons the bees,
The death-bees, to be fed with it?
This is the terrible curse of men and trees,
To tear their loveliness and gods deep out of them,
Lift them to skies and heavenly Edens far out of reach,
Weep in their own wildernesses, die in their own deserts.
The trees of evening have too little of the moon they love
But bear the darkness like the fruit of night.

The heavy plunging branches cannot rise above
The sea of shadows. The moon and all her loyal stars
Walks like the exiled monarch of a lesser light
Upon the waters of the dark, and we are no more trees
But the mysterious depths of danger.
Hope dies with dawn. Day breaks and is
The seal of our discouragement, for what is plain
Is clasped within the prison of what it is.
And has a man much more? The silver of his hopes
Reposes in the gray of terror weary.
Beauty will bear him many children with sweet souls
But tainted bodies since he must be their frantic father."

Oh, I can sing a man my life's amazed lament,
And tristfully apart a tree sobs to a tree.
This is the living kiss of each to his own kind.
But afterwards, but in the long and passionate death,
I will forever make the sore sign of our common woe.
I shall be restless with my love of grief and go
Kissing the cold lips of all the trees my moan can find.

A Preface

Come to me for truth:
      The moon is so and so.
      The earth is what it is.
      Rivers and lies have deep bottoms.
      Nothing is ever anything else
      And everything is what we think it is.

Come to me for understanding.
      I will tell you:
      Things are because of this and that to-day.

And then come back again to-morrow.

Another's Tongue

The tongue of another
Is as the sun.
It speaks and swelters,
Would scorch wagging like a Phaëthon
And blister the enlightened ear,
Make Eros an Ethiopian,

Without the serpent in its slime
Contemplative and cool did often
Lie in a dumbness and a dark,
Breed in the bog a spirit sometime
Of shame and silence.

So we hear but the half of any sermon
And know as our own sleep only
The night where the proud blade is bitten,
Pinched and hunched in the narrow cell
Where without lips speech confesses
It is an alternate in turn
Of quiet.

Be anxious then to hear
With mouth as well as ear,
Attend another's tongue
Choking on your own.

Let it inflame you as little
As your own can burn in its own spittle.
Or, if it fly too ardent at you,
Feel in your own deep throat
How both are safe,
How it is fastened.

Appearances

Let me stand wondering on a hilltop.

The trees are silent princesses
Proud of their tall virginity
And yet regretting roots
And happy that their branches
Are less chaste than they.

The songs of birds climb upon low clouds
That bear them quietly to their echoes
Waiting behind me in the valley.

A little river stitches its way
Into the earth untidily.
Silence lies enchanted in the woods whispering.

What shall I say of those
Who come aspiring underneath my hilltop,
Plumed with hope:

Children like primroses,
Knowing that primroses would be fairer than myself
Upon a hilltop,
Golden with sun and primroses.

And women are winds,
Restive and envious of my repose.
And men are rocks,
Envious, too,
That I should be so frail and high
And vigorous and light upon a hill.

What am I, then, above all these?
A pinnacle for dreams,
A wavering sign,
A tower built of all the things that are not.

Do not mock me,
That I seem to forget the nature of things,
Giving them strange names,

Finding virginity in trees,
And songs wrapped up in clouds,
Calling the rivers threads
And children primroses
And women winds
And men rocks
And myself a pinnacle for dreams.

For I can remember the time
When I was not fancying upon a hill
And knew as well as you and anyone
That trees are only trees
And everything other than itself.

Yet – how shall I tell you –
From my watchtower I have made discoveries
And perceived the unapparent dreams of things
Added to each small sum,
Making it great beyond itself –
What but a dream has lifted me so tall upon a hilltop?

You who are so wise,
You who are like a tree yourself,
Planted in truth and unwalking,
You can tell me much of trees
And what trees are made of.
There is none as learned as yourself
In the ways of birds and rivers
And children and women and men,
In the things of which they are made
And the things into which they shall turn,
Knowing why a bird may rest firmly upon soft air
And a river ripples upon its bed
And people creep into old age unaware,
As if it were a shell, and die.

You who are so wise –
What can you tell me of their dreams?

You who mock me in the valley –
How shall I deny that I am mounted only on a dream?

And yet – you who are so shrewd
For counting all the little bones of reality –
Who are you to know
Whether I am awake or asleep?

Beauty Is Kind

Beauty is kind
To choose this way
Of matter and mind
For her array,
To be thus shown
Through paint and pen,
Nor prized alone
But loved in men,
Doomed to compete
With skies and trees
And other sweet
Accessories.

Beauty is kind
To be so trimmed
And risk to find
Her glory dimmed
With lesser grace.
Yet what risk we,
What sorrow face,
If true it be
Beauty were not
So celebrate
If she forgot
To decorate?

Bereavement

Who will there be, life, when I am gone?
Who will be as I am,
A wave unto you, fierce and high-crested,
Sharpest rift and ridge of you?

You will never have another to be as I was,
Tall and mounted above you
And yet one to rest on you again,
Tinily, tenderly,
Leaving not even the fold of a ripple
Where I had once climbed up on you,
Impetuously arched, calling myself free,
Arched and bent loyally back toward you again.

It is not for myself, life,
That I grieve that I shall die,
But for you.
That there will be no other,
No child for your old age
To whisper to deaf ears
And luminously see for clouded eyes.

What have I not been for you –
A wave fierce and high-crested
Above your unaspiring plain;
A fingertip to lay upon yourself
And feel your own unwitting passion;
A song that you may hear the sound of your own voice
And know how swift and rapturous you are.

You will grieve for me, life.
You will grow dim and unaware
And there will be no other messenger
To bring you tidings of yourself,
Some wistful testimony that you are at all.

You will go running, running down the years,
Not knowing what you seek.
But it will be yourself
That you have lost in losing me,

And I shall not be there to help you find
Us both.

These things I am telling you now, life,
Knowing still how soon I shall be sent away.
For you can never learn
How much I shall be missed, until I die,
When there will be
No one to speak for you and me. Or if there is,
Yet will it be too late to call me back.

But What of Trees?

There are no jewels now to cover up
The cruelly knotted fingers of the trees
All taut to clutch the white throat of the sky
And claw the sunset with ambitious hands
That grimly hunger over beauty's head.
Their longing is a scythe that silently
At nightfall hangs athirst to mow the dark
As if the stars were made for reaping-time.

There are those who are free and yet go gloved
With hands fit only for demure self-clasping
That would not reach to gather anything.
The ways they go are bare and dry with sand –
Not even a satyr could leave a footprint there,
Nor would it stir for any growing thing
Were these indeed the feet to quicken it.

But what of trees with feet that may not walk?
If they were free to go abroad, who knows
What majesty would nobly tread the earth
And what new magic for bewilderment
Would spring up at their feet, if they were free?

There are those who are free to love and yet,
When all is done, nothing is left beyond
A hate or some thin memory that has
Grown weary of a long remembering.

But what of trees if they were free to love?
What rare and unencompassed little thing
Might come of their embrace, could they once meet?

But Wickedness . . .

It is not for itself
That I love wickedness.
But wickedness has such sweet ways!

Thieves walk at night
And make the night more silent.

Murderers love madness
And a moment's high courage for killing.
It is not that I love killing,
But good men soften in their sanity
And smile too frequently.

Cruelty has a thousand charms.
Pain is a beauty lashed upon my back.
Oh, why is mercy kind?
Oh, why is justice blind,
Too blind for punishment?

Evil has as many enchantments as the night.
Lies are as mysterious as the stars.
The moon is a new truth each night
And shadows gamble for the moon dishonestly,
While goodness stays at home behind drawn blinds,
Hiding her beauty in a prayer,
Correctly wived to a monk's hood.
And will not lie or love or dream.

If goodness loosed her hair
And danced at night with danger,
If goodness were as lovely half as sin,
I'd husband goodness then for her own sake
And find a thousand charms in virtue.

But wickedness has such sweet ways!

Cadence for an Elegy

If you pass my house at night
You will say:
It is a dark house to have no light.
It is a many-windowed house
To be so silent to those who pass.

You should have come at dusk,
Gently peering at dusk
Before the candles are blown,
Before their nervous little heads
Are blown upon the pillows of darkness.

You would have said:
It is a bright house,
But the shadows stooping behind the windows
Are like the sadness
Veiling the maiden eyes of a young mother.
It is a many-windowed house
That one should sit spinning in it with her eyes to the wall.
It is a great house
That she should sit spinning with her eyes to the wall
In a little room at the top
That trembles to the sunset
Like a frail girl before a strong lover.

Do not envy me my watch-tower
In the house of my disconsolateness.
It is the peak of sombre days
And there are only
The slow steps of my hopes to mount it.

Do not envy me my wall.
I have seen too much from windows.
I have built my house
With what is wanly seen from windows.
It is tall enough now,
Tall enough for toppling.

Do not envy me my wheel.
It grows more stubborn with each turning.
But oh, how indurately spun
My cerements will be.

See – he comes!
The steps of my hopes sing beneath his tread.
One feathery touch of his upon my wheel –

One cool, light minute of spring
Matched against a season of summer
Heavy with fragrance and warm breezes –

One moment of his
Delicately, amorously leaning
Against my seriously builded years –
As one inch of heaven would have tumbled
That tower once devised in Shinar
And spared the common tongue,
If it had not been visited
By God's improvident, early indignation –

Oh my dark temple!
It was for this I raised you so carefully.

Oh pleasant ruins!
Go ferreting there some kindly night.
Rake the clutter daintily
With the fingers of your memory.
You will find a wheel.
Leave it.
It is too worn for a new turning,
And the spindle is unwound.

You will find nearby
The little white tiles of my steps.
Perhaps they will be whole and shimmering yet,
For I kept them clean and well mended.
Take them!
They are my hopes,
And I have no need of them now.

Callando

Every day I went to hear Callando speak.
For his voice was the small hushed echo
Of some unheard and larger sound
And I was young and fond of mysteries.

I fluttered shyly to the ground
And wrapped my scarf against his seriousness,
Crying: "Old man, speak
And tell me again what life is
That I may laugh
And prove that it isn't anything at all
But an old man like yourself, Callando,
With thin legs bent merrily beneath him
And a forehead foolish with wrinkles and solemnity,
And a boy like myself,
Smirched with manhood
Like a clean birch spotted with black bark."

Once I went to him and threw myself at his feet
And said: "Callando, the sky is as near as ever
And I think I saw a bird fly into it
And not come out again
And I have forgotten all that you told me yesterday."

Called Death

Limp he hung in the flabby forestate,
A leap across to stand stiff,
A soft thud on the threshold and a whiff
As a backbone from above would plumb him
Osteal in the new place.
But his mucid mind shuddered,
His clammy skin rippled.
He could not flow in as he would have loved,
As loose and lacteous as the door were a dam
Or slip over in a slimy skiff.
He must solid across and keen
A groin and an arm-pit in the going
And collect an eye where the sluggish liquid
Flickered a light, was bright
Of its own refraction inbent
And both ways beautiful
In sight made visible.

Yet come he could not nuclear
Nor was allowed in less than life
The black love of the sweets of suicide
To flatter despair with fear.
It was a hand at last that rescued him
With hungry phalanges distent in the webless fan
Flying five separate trails upon him.

Mother merciful raked her babe together,
Clawed her pet across the sharp sill
Losing not a doubtful drop,
For Father had wildly kissed every finger
Over and over well until cruel.

Limp no longer; he will have milk,
He will have marrow, grieve heavier
Into an upright skeleton and a soul,
Stiffen painful and proud and tighten
Into the fastened frame out of which
May be no unscrewing but is wisest now
In this jostling to be pinned against.

Spryly he sprints now, having forgotten
In his easy joints how his mother made him
With his father's help.
Up and down now clambers the whelp
Discovering heaven in his eye
Where a sudden crook of sight seems high,
And love later in his fingers feeling
Still another alive, quivering
More and more steady,
Less and less liquid,
Less and less body.
He and a strange lady suffer, stand upright,
Inure and martyrize to air.
It is the last state and the longest
Of stalwart skeleton and pure form,
Of frame with flesh unimpeded
And life because livelier
Called death.

Ceremonial

I shall bow three times
    In meeting.
I shall hate you correctly
    For greeting.

I shall kiss you each night,
    Proper and cool.
I shall keep my tongue neat and dry
    Your love to befool.

I shall polish my smile,
    Saluting your banners
With trim amiability
    And courteous manners.

I shall bow three times
    When we part,
Having murdered politely
    Your heart.

Conclusion

Some part of me is ever away
Faring in fields where something grows –
There's nowhere any but me that knows
The terrible herb I press each day
Into a bitter that never ran
So savory in another man.

What absent mood that keeps me fed
And moves the heart within the brute
Will one day gather the last root
And I'll be hungering and dead
Because some part of me comes back
Without the healing draught I lack?

When none of me can live to roam,
The wandering witch in me that found
A dram abroad to keep me sound
May yet discover a weed at home
To nourish and revive the rest
Of that in me I never guessed.

Cordelia

Cordelia's needle had been stitching since
An unforgotten time when there had been
A hope to labor for and all her dreams
Were bridges swung to truths poignantly peaked
With half-perceived and tall delights enwrapped
In time. And when that little word had come
All innocent of what it lightly brought,
To tell her of his death as would a child
Unwittingly and winsomely discourse
Of serious things, she only smiled and spoke
Of small adjustments to be made until
The truths were fragile bridges all festooned
With streamers from the banks they intertwined,
These banks that once were truths and now were dreams.

And so she twisted saffron in her gown
And curled her hair to titillate her ears
And then crept coyly to her bed to dream
Her wedding day. So for a year she sewed
Until that chest incrusted once with shy
And modest bridal things, now whispered to
A miniature attire for a desire
As yet undreamed, while neighbors watched her sew
And blush as young wives will for secrets that
Are bashfully revealed through all their sweet
Timidity and said, "Poor thing, her grief
Has turned Cordelia daft," not knowing that
Cordelia had no grief but only dreams
And nighttimes that were luminous not for
Their stars but for the days she lived in them
That might have been, and they were dearer yet
That they were not, and all more likely for
That chest that fattened with new clothes and toys
And tokens for a fond maternity
And fonder wifehood yet, like some deceived
Imagined memory invented to
Invest a worried past with spurious
Enchantments. So she sewed now pinafores
All pert with starch and sturdy knickers for
A romping lad. At Christmas-tide were gifts
Of sober-sprigged cravats for John and once
A pipe since John was getting old and fond
Of firesides and a sled for Ted and dolls
For Agatha; some birthday favors, too,
Affectionately tumbled in that chest
To be a testimony of that life
That she had lived mysteriously beyond
Her distant actual days. And she had need
Of argument quite soon enough, for one
Remembering day there came a word from John
To her to say that he had never died
But only treacherously run away
And that his infidelity had found
A penitent old age and that he must
Come back to her or die unpardoned of
Himself. But if she would forgive him, he
Would have the punishment he merited.

20

Cordelia only shook her head and smiled
Incredulously while she lifted up
The cover of her chest and wisely said
With trusting certainty, "Oh, I am sure
It cannot be, here's John's old muffler that
I made him many years ago, and there
I see Fred's skates and Agatha's blue sash.
We'll have to send this letter back again
And say there must be some mistake because
My John was never dead and never ran
Away." And those who heard her only said
It was a blessing that she had gone mad,
Nor saw when they had gone what sober tears
Were rimmed in rational eyes for a sane moment.

Cricket's Spring

The hammocks of the cricket's shrill
Rock the tired spring,
Reward the day that meek and still
Loves not to sing

At all, while less unflattering
Night climbs the hill
And, as the dozing hammocks swing
·Slumber and fill
The silence with the music summer makes
If young enough in spring, it wakes
The sun and whispers, faltering
With light, the vernal compliment
A wretched pride on the ascent
Of dawn scrapes from a cricket's wing.

Dawn

Dawn comes, is dawn and flees again.
I am a dawn that grows
From day into a dark repose
Where in the crowded night of Pain

Doubt edges in too narrowly
Along the margin of my tent
Of dreams, breaking discouragement
Upon to-morrow's dawn of me.

Did I Not Die?

Did I not die yesterday, when –
Who asks?
I ask.
I am alive, then.

Why was I not still?
Another could have as easily
Proceeded with my story.
Haven't I had my fill
Of human glory?

Where is God?

Must I wait until
God has had his fill?

Dilemma

Beloved of many, yet loving none herself,
If she could find something to pay·them with
That might impoverish her enough to seem
Love's substitutes, she might succeed with this
Pretense of gratitude in fostering
The sacrificial mood of abnegation,

22

Forswearing the inducements of a proud
Indebtedness and free at last to treat
With love itself, where she might find it, not
Aware of her, but growing in a garden,
Where she might pick it, smell it, throw it down
And crush it and have done with it for good.
But love seemed too involved in flesh to use
This way, nor yet could she discover what
The coin might be that would negotiate
The importuning claims of those who loved
Her. Hate might have acquitted her, but hate
Was but the other pole of love. And death
Had left them all remembering, unpaid.
Here is a lady truly cruel, but caught
In a predicament of kindliness.

Divestment

See how I am like a tree, beloved.
See how I am garrulous with leaves.

For I have chattered nervously all spring,
Glib and gushing as a young girl.

In the summer I was a matron.
I learned to talk less wisely then.

But I would not be silent in autumn.
Even my fallen leaves became echoes.

Be a wind, beloved.
Tear out each little wagging tongue
        Till I am stark,
        Till I am mute.

        For I cannot say no
        To you then, beloved.

Doomed

Wear out at last, old earth,
Sold and sold over.
The spires will never fly or break
Or man cease ever for your sake,
Resting the rover
Or letting life stop death and birth.

No peace can come a time between,
Each covenanter
Only of bitter dreams of war
That each fears finding reason for.
Man is no scanter
Because of earth, earth no less green

For all the green man has torn out
And trampled under.
Hate can but this intolerable be
Where hate can find no injury
To pardon plunder
Hate unaggrieved must do without.

Wear out then both and say
The truce is broken
That peace or war had neither kept,
Only some terror that has slept
Upon the token
That both must die on the same day.

Earth, Great Eyeball

Earth, great eyeball,
Hear me, of the parasites that crawl
Speckling on you: Do you see
The same sun as blinds me?
Or is my blackest most your blackest
And my loveliest light your meanest?

Yet, mirror-deep in you, am I not beheld
On a horizon, though a speck, swelled
To be a man in your vision
With a multiple eye of my own?
This is sight, then: a distance in the pain,
How the mind removes its own profane
By a retirement, enriched in every scourge
Dappling naked sense. Light can emerge
Where it cannot come in. Darkness can be
The light by which we see.
Earth has us in her eye astray,
Like love thinks very far away
And loses us among her skies.
Heaven is a pensiveness that flies
Out of Eden, breaks the marge
Of space, dreams us large
As man from the mites we were
Besetting and blinding her.
The plague is banished not by plucking out
The eye with its infection, but roundabout
Is best for both. We are sight
In the great ball. We are light
In our own souls and live,
As well as earth, by the grace we give
The tyranny of body and breath
Whose endurance is an endurance of death.

Epigrams

Because of men and women there is love.
Because of love there still are men and women.
Passion may be the knife that makes them two.
Passion yet knits them into one again.
Aimless is life whose aim is not all love.
Aimless is love that leads not into life.
The need is full the answer of desire.
The need that asks for more gets only strife.
If we set love to labor love will go.
If we must toil for love love will not come.

Love that recalls the start looks toward the end.
Love that is too much sung will soon be dumb.
Love that is left to sleep and hold its breath,
Love such as this will wake to weep in death.

Evasions

Streets move evasively and so do people.
Both chew their covert cuds and yet they are
Quite different. For streets have consciences
At street-corners and spit their cuds there at
The curb with lamp-posts for confessors.

But people only swallow theirs and go
To hide in houses, fearing edges and
Sharp turnings that might bring them face to face
With unexpected honesties or yet
A sudden crying ordinance to halt
Their apprehensive slinking in the streets
And call them fiercely to encounters there
With one another's eyes and ponderings.

And yet, because they go so nervously
And do not stop for scrutiny, shall we
Call caution furtiveness or rather say
That shunning candor, they find sanity.

For Those Who Stay Up at Night

Busy, busy,
Turn, turn.
God keeps his wheels blowing,
Blowing and breaking the wind all day,
Breaking the wind into bits of breezes....

Busy, busy, –
And each of us is the hub of a wheel,
The heart of a wheel
For God's turning.
(Spokes won't make the wheel go.)

God strokes the rim.
Spokes tread on swiftness
And try to catch each other.
The hub goes round,
Catching glimpses of windy wheeling,
Piecing and patching glimpses to living.

Turn, turn,
Busy, busy,
Round, round,
The day is not over.
God works at his cartwheels:
A rim and some spokes
And the hub of each of us.

Slow, slow,
Weary, weary.
God stops turning.
The wind won't be ground on wheels again
Till to-morrow.

(When wheels go round
Hubs piece and patch a sun to-gether
From the sparks of their speed.
But weary, weary,
God stops turning.
Stillness takes the sun apart.
Swiftness will put it together again
In the morning.)

Quiet, quiet,
Night nothing,
Hubs dreaming
Of day-turning.

Who will not sleep at night?
Who keeps God busy
Turning, turning,
Faster, faster.
Perhaps a moon can be put together
And a couple of stars?

Sometimes not enough stay up at night
To put anything more than the dark together.

Sometimes nobody stays up at all –
Night nothing,

Hubs dreaming
Of day-turning.

Does God ever rest?
Does God ever sleep?
Does God ever forget?

You who stay up at night,
Keep watching, keep watching,
Sleepless, sleepless,
God will keep turning,
Faster, faster....

God may grow tired,
God may forget....

Keep watching,
Keep watching....

Forbidden

"– republican and democrat.
I never should have thought, my friend,
That you could be as wrong as that."

"And do you think I bear a mote
In my mind's eye that I'd depend
On your opinion for my vote?"

"Hush, for I think the night debars
Discussion. It never could be so still
If we taught politics to stars."

Harlequinade on a Curbstone

The Blind Man is sitting on a carriage stone near the curb. His
head is bald, clown-like. His cane has a crooked handle and has
been hung upon his belt like a sword. His face is so white, that
were it not for the rest of him, you would be quite sure by now
that he *was* a clown. His left leg is resting on the curb, while the
other has been drawn up on the carriage stone. This leg he is
hugging with clasped hands, leaning his face upon the knee so
that he seems rather to be dreaming than unseeing. At his left,
sitting on the curb, is his companion, a boy of nineteen. He is
very proud of his wise young eyes and his legs are sprawled into
the gutter as if to halt passing vehicles. They sit very quietly for
several seconds without saying anything. Then the Blind Man
turns himself a little toward the boy. As he does so, an old hag
slinks out of the darkness and sits down on the curb to the right
of the Blind Man, without noticing him. At first she sits with her
head hung over her breast and her legs sprawled into the gutter
like the Blind Man's boy. But when she realizes that the Blind
Man and his companion are talking about her, she facetiously
attempts to imitate the appearances and gestures he describes.

The Blind Man. Someone is sitting there, Gamaliel.
The Boy. Why, by your sight, and so there is and yet
If you were not a man to see with some
Unerring sense what my provided sockets
Perceive with a misgiving for their sight,
I should be sure that what I see is but
A trick of tired beholding, for my eyes
Have labored for the both of us and so
Are doubly weary for their twofold task.

29

B.M. But tell me then, Gamaliel, who sits
So quietly beside us on the curb.
I think it was a woman whom I heard –
Her skirt was like a ripple on the street.
Boy. We'll call her that. I wish there was a name
More fair or yet no name at all, that I
Might fashion one of those forgotten, sweet,
Uncommon letters not confided to
The alphabet.
B.M.   Is she so lovely, then?
Boy. If you could see – forgive me – how her feet
Are poised obliquely on her little heels –
Her eyes, if they are half as limpid as
Her tears, I'd be afraid to look in them
On a dark night like this. Tell me, did you
Once peer into a woman's eyes that you
Have grown so blind?
B.M.   So she is weeping, boy?
Boy. Ah, how she weeps – divine dregs for a gutter,
A naiad come to mourn her tainted stream
And wind her hair –
B.M.   But what then of her hair?
Boy. Her forehead is a white and laughing joy
Her hair is wrapped about it like a grief –
B.M. Say "winding sheet".
Boy.   Well, winding sheet. Her nose –
B.M. Let's leave that out.
(The old hag, who was about to show her nose in profile, makes
a gesture of disappointment.)
        Her mouth?
Boy.   Her lips are silk
To the smooth lips of night, more silken to
The night than that soft gown of hers to this
Unyielding, obdurate curb – those little lips
That somehow seem to say –
B.M.   Don't tell, I know:
(Now the streets become dun with lamplight. The chimneypots
of the house behind them are suddenly visible, like two ears
pricked to attention. As the Blind Man sings his song the old hag
gets up and dances to the tune.)
        The moon is a widow,
        The plump-faced bald moon.

For I've murdered the night
And the day'll be here soon.
(The Blind Man gets up, makes a deep bow to the gutter and
then sits down on the curb to finish his song, using his cane as
a baton.)

        Roundelay, roundelay,
        Hear my ridiculous roundelay.

        The faithful old moon will
        Not marry the day,
        So he marries the sun
        To the poor moon's dismay.

        Roundelay, roundelay,
        What a ridiculous roundelay.

        The sun is a widow,
        She's stored up her pelf.
        No I've not killed the day.
        She killed him herself.

        Roundelay, roundelay,
        Oh, my ridiculous roundelay.

        To marry but one
        Of these widows I'm loath.
        I'd much rather be, though,
        A lover to both.

        Roundelay, is it now
        Such a ridiculous roundelay.
(Here the old hag laughs and stops dancing and goes back to the
curb again, still chuckling.)

      B.M. This woman is a little mad, I think.
      Boy. She must be mad to bear us company.
      B.M. Is she such a great lady, then, a queen
      Perhaps?
      Boy.   Not quite a queen, I'm sure.
      B.M.   Perhaps
      A princess then, at least?
(Here a policeman appears at the left.)
      Boy.   Not quite. She seems

To be a duchess. Only duchesses
Would have the grace to be a little mad
And hobnob with blind beggars and their boys.
Policeman. Away now, you there.
B.M.   Who is that?
Boy.   Why that's
The Duke. He's come to fetch his wife and lead
Her back to that great palace just behind.
(The old hag walks off in the manner of a duchess, followed by
the policeman who once more motions to the Blind Man and his
companion to move on.)
    B.M. Well, come, and let's go hunting princesses
To-morrow and a queen next week and then
We'll have to search a fortnight or perhaps
A fortnight of fortnights until we come
Upon a driveling old hag, for they,
I've learned, my boy, are very hard to find.

Heed

All those who know each other too well, –
Where the mists have lifted,
Where the sight is straight,
Never losing itself in a dream,
But riding from halo to halo
And hate to hate, –
Turn away,
Turn away from the brightest gleam.
The utmost vision is blindness.
Turn away before the last enlightened moment.
Death is the final wisdom.
Turn away and forget in the shadow,
You two
And all others who know each other too well.

Turn again, some day,
Dim and remembering,
Take your hands from your eyes,
Cry across the dusk, half-listening,

Moving in separate dark,
Faintly aware how love travels between you,
Back and forth across a fen of misunderstanding,
Groping and sure, looking not up to see,
Lest it lose itself.

Her Portion

Having as much of pain as she can hold,
Can she be blamed for giving to another
That which her heart, too full already, spills?
She feels no more the pass of love's quick flood.
Still in the perfect mold her memories
Lie wakeful, while beyond the careful brim,
Just out of compass, where forgetting starts,
Sleep waits for her in case she should regret
The even share, agree to hold too much, and break.

Heraclea
(To Alastor)

She called, Heraclea,
Sang across space shrouded
With love like a heroic age,
Clouded to be remembered, because too bright.

He was no more than a weak warrior of the Hesperides,
But golden, golden....
His sword gleamed out of a tree,
His heart shone through his breast,
Never a warrior but he
Could conquer her unrest,
Turn the torrid noon of her
To a twilight of summer.

Eavesdropping on the sea,
Marking the tidal echoes of the land,
She knew he would come neither way,
Not faithless but afraid.

Then, in her need,
Out of a seed of hopelessness,
Heraclea bore her warrior
To death and bore him brave;
While on the shore of the Hesperides
A living ghost sank into the sand,
Afraid to battle for his grave.

How Can I Die

How can I die
When I have kept my beauty bare
For sorrow and for merriment
And worn a flower in my hair
To be a fair acknowledgement
What things may die?

How can I die
When I have been so rapturous
To be alive and feel the sun
And am my self's own Pegasus
Forever plighted to outrun
All things that die?

Yet I shall die.
For I have loved this life and been
A giver of young reverence.
Eternity bides only in
A resolute indifference
To things that die.

Yet I shall die.
Time will endure through my despair.
She takes me for an ornament
And wears me gayly in her hair
To be a fair acknowledgement
What things may die.

How Does a Tree...

How does a tree hold up the sky
Better than I?
How is a tree happier under the load?

Ah, what does a tree know?
The leaves look up,
The roots run down,
And the way from the farthest leaf to the farthest root
Is the same way back again.

But a body buries its tongue in the earth,
Is a long time singing it up to the sky,
But only a terrible minute
Waiting for it to fall silently down again.

What can a tree tell of trouble,
Sure and straight between two tips,
The spar of the earth
And the staff of the sky?

But a man, but a man,
Caught and crying over the earth and under the sky
Has a head to mind how heavy they are
And to know how he's crippled and crushed between.

In the City of Grim Streets...

In the City of Grim Streets,
In the city where the shadows do not move,
And life is a little still rain
And death the sun that dries it up again,
Send me my Lady of Sorrow,
With her face veiled
And her candle unlit.

I shall make her a silent welcome at the gate
And light the candle
And draw the veil
And lead her home as my quiet bride.

Then will there be one heart elate
In the City of Grim Streets,
In the city where the shadows do not move.

Interval

Fandra, Fandra, love him not.
Look not his way so often,
Looking up only to find a star
And see him quickly after,
Not for comparison, I'm sure,
But to approach him starwise....

Fandra, Fandra, love him not.

"Lethal gardens,
Flowers of danger...."
He used to say,
Dreaming, remembering, forgetting
Tempests he had been quiet in,
Seas that had hated him
For loving them too well to be afraid of them,
High encounters with the desperation of fate
Against his quaint enchantment....

Ancient in peace, secure, unsmiling,
Untired, untouched, experienced,
He came back saying,
"Lethal gardens,
Flowers of danger....
Maybe love will find me an injury
To stir and sadden and wither the heart at last."

But Fandra, Fandra!
Don't look.
Don't go.
He can't be hurt.
I know.

Careless and unimpaired,
He's saying now,
"Lethal gardens,
Flowers of danger
Bloom and fade,
Bloom and fade,
Imperil themselves
But bitter not me."

"Lethal gardens,
Flowers of danger....
Fortunate fragrance....
....fade....fade"

Fandra!
Fandra....

Still, blossoming there was sweet.

Fandra, wait!
Fasten your gown with this.
It may remind him how –
Maybe he'll put you in my old place....

Ah, Fandra,
Wait.
Don't go.

Invocation for Birds

Mists of our blindness, something be,
Be birds, we have no birds this spring.
We were busy with a new year
In our breasts.
Birds have always been.
Why are nests
This year denuded, if we forgot,
And mists up over memories
Flying lightning wingless
That will not strike?
The year was made to pass quickly,
It was too quick for birds,
We flew too fast for flight,
We lost a brightness, we lost the birds,
The sun-translating sounds
Of evening and the voice of dawn
To pry sleep open narrowly,
Give the day entrance where
Quiet choked black, was too unutterable.
And we have only mists fluttering the skies
Close, mists only in our eyes
Impossible of tears, of birds.
The blindness goes immense
Into the cavernous groves of the new year
At the earth's pulse dumb,
An old earth speeding vainly.
It is a grave and ghastly
To be buried in our own dust, in our own darkness.
Our hearts have mated with naked vultures
Behind us and hatched a brood of mists,
Brought hell on us nearly a loveliness,
Heaven nearly, but birdless.

Mists, be birds again, as always.
What are birds, that we have lost them
For a sin of haste, for too fast a flourish
Forward to an age that may be death overtaken?
Is it death already blinking in our sight
Nature out of countenance?

A stride of steel walks the warm savagery
Of miracles under foot and cold.
Our eyes shudder of a self-horror.
We have begotten engines upon fright,
Are commandeered by the Eumenides
Of an immortal hunger in our mortal mouths.
They have our bleeding eyes,
Beat our brains high in Tartarus.
Our sense is wakeful with the Maidens
Where they brave the Fates, are fierce
Against the signs of pity in us
For what ourselves were, weaker.

But another bravery dreams like love
Back to last year's birds,
Swims in the eyes with mists
That may be nothing but our sight's sorrow,
Under the sentence of too much inwardness,
To know where the birds still lead
And we might follow
South and slow
Less deathless but less dangerously.
The mists are false, float songless.
What if the grass is gone next year
For fresher wisdoms and an ethereal
Of mad gray pane thinks under us
And the year after we are ourselves
An iron breath
Clanging hell's breath terribler
With such inspirited breath,
We are as more than live,
Thus bodiless?

Mists, give us back our eyes,
The birds in them, the bright
And faithful flight
Humble to get heaven not too soon,
Bounding the same height each year over
But staring stronger
Into the sun, until the eyes behold
Where the ancient globe and gold
Flew torrid to creation,

Put life a faith in eyes and wings to prove
Heaven is what is highest seen and flown
Of the strange heritage alterable
Only if some dark spite and hell
Starts blindness and oblivion
A year or century too soon
By freeing death of bondage in the head
Where demons smoke up mists
To do for birds when light is dead.

Jazz Jubilate

I
The Blind Beggar in the Back Street

Make a joyful noise unto the Lord all ye lands.
Tune up the Tiger,
Ruffle up the proud silk Tiger of the backwoods,
The lonely, the only.
The bright brown prowling
Cruel brave soul.
Bring it out.
Tame it down.
Tune it up.
Lord, make my beast a loving lamb.
Lord, lead my pet, my scowling baby
Out of the jungle
Into the light.
It'll gulp down the gloom.
Only give it room.
Give it music.
Give it whiskey
Till it's frisky.
Let me ride my sweet devil all over the world.
We'll gobble up the ground,
Pull out the earth from under their feet.
Who's afraid of the air?
Who's afraid of the Lord?
Listen to that melody

Driving out your doldrums,
Frightening the goblins,
Warming up your frozen toes.
Wriggle them free,
Join the jubilee.
Can't you see
The happy spirit shining through the clouds
And the holy angels dancing out in crowds?
Can't you hear
The big brass band that beats in everybody's heart
And in everybody's land
Jollying disaster,
Teasing time faster,
Warming up the blood,
Drying up the flood,
Pounding up the earth,
Digging up the mirth
For the whole blessed mob,
The dizzy dozens stepping
Lively to heaven?

II
Mother of Pearl Palace

The wax shines brightly
On the ballroom floor nightly,
Starts the corybantic chemistry,
No introductions necessary.
Trot-trot-trot,
See a lady Hottentot
Hobnobbing with an ambassador
Along the slippery floor.
The spectacular spree of democracy
Is very cheery, also eerie.
It's a terribly believable dream that hypnotizes
The hilarious bones while the flesh atomizes
And the spirit sweeps in,
The great aloof spirit –
Can't you hear it
Humming and whistling the syncopated romance
Of the free-for-all dance?

41

O if you want to fly
And get to heaven before you die,
You must believe in your body,
Give it a chance
To prove the spirit alive,
To dissolve in the dance
And gallop like a ghostly mare
Along the everlasting track
Hoofing a horse-shoe prayer
For the soul on its back.

III
Sunday

Reverend Cobbleweb withdrew to his study
Sunday evening after prayers.
His boots were mild and muddy
Of irreligious roads, blind toads, too,
Tripping up his reveries the whole way home
With devils in disguises
And splashes and surprises.

But at home he had slippers,
Such slippers stitched by Mrs.,
The toes tucked deep away,
The heels adhering hard
And sensible of the Lord –
The toes tucked deep away
Too dark to play
On Sunday evening when the Reverend
Rested in his study, smoked a pipeful to God.
Most mysterious his mood
As manifested in Cobbleweb,
Not irreverent not serious
Somewhat frolic somewhat fierceness:
"Lord, what is it?
I can't resist it.
Is it sin?"
God continues to grin
And Reverend Cobbleweb's slippers slough off.
The toes have light.

The smile incarcerated in the scowl
Comes bright
And even beautiful.
Bare feet, bare face – how worshipful
Is joy. There is a pact of revelry not reverie
Now under way,
God gay in his parson,
Parson gay in his God:
"Clear the floor,
Close the door,
Come in, Big Brother,
We have business together.
It's the same old sermon
That I dribbled out to my darling congregation,
But I'm delivering it to you
Dear God without the spew,
Without my clerical collar
Choking thick my throat:
Less than a dollar
To squeeze my Adam's apple
Compact into my gullet.
But it wasn't meant for quiet.
It was meant to wiggle,
It was meant to gargle,
It was meant to be kept rolling
Happy in its spittle.
Kiss me lord, where you hear my neck rattle.
Love's not music, love's not beauty,
And my body has grown bony
Creaking how it loves you.
Big Brother kiss me
Where I'm hoarse holloing you.

There's a devil cavorting in me
When I don't cavort.
There's a bloody issue in my heart
Where they won't let me bellow.
Lord, they want their prayers yellow.
Lord, they want a fellow
To freeze up their fires,
Make heavens of their hells
With the Sunday blues and bells.

43

Lord, save me. I'll be bile
In a little while
If you don't find a use for me, mount me
Make an ass of me, mount me,
Ride me to Jerusalem
Braying love loud through the sickly crowd,
Dancing you, Boss,
Up to the Cross,
To the top of the ladder.
Lord, later and sadder
I'll carry you home through the startled gates singing
Singing both the same thanksgiving,
Dear Brother, for each other."

Reverend Cobbleweb suffered of a madness
Tired and perspired Sunday evening in his study
Snoring upstairs, resting after prayers,
Stretching his ten nippers in his slippers,
Wheezing while his throat felt better
Uncockled by a collar,
Gurgling: "Come before the Lord with gladness:
Come before his presence singing."

IV
Lady Love and the Ladies

Lady Love, Lady Love,
Art every man's love
And every man's ewe?
Lady Love, Lady Love,
What do you do
So white and wooly
Grazing, nozzling lambkin,
Where hearts are green and hilly,
Where hearts are high and lonely
To be coddled, nozzled, nosed,
Made pasture, made rapture
With everlasting mercy
To eyes with lamb's wool closed,
To eyes that doze in rose
Unless they blink with white,

44

Cottony and comatose,
Where green heart grows
To hillocks and the billows
Break and blossom for Heaven's Lady –
Oh no, not Mary!
Mary is too proud
To come down in a cloud
Foaming full
With lamb's wool.
Mary is not brave.
God's mistress cannot save
The rams from the regimen
Of modern women.
Only God's laughter bleating in his daughter
Plaintive as a lamb
To please any plain ram
Sanctifies the mystery
Softly and lovingly
Of sheepishness in history,
In men principally,
When maids grow too modern,
See too clear and sudden,
And God needs to be a woman
Eyes down in the grass,
True lamb and lass
Parading to the prayer and serenading,
Nibbling herbs that blossom to her bosom,
Giving love out in wool
So silk and beautiful,
The hills ascend
The way four lamb's feet wend
Skipping stars up to heaven
Where there are no women
But a Lady Love dwells
In the den of a lion
Bleating heaven's bells
In lambs and dithyrambs.

Dionysus, too, in other climes,
Has chimes,
And modern women know a way to Tartarus
Down-dancing to the tinkling

Of a lamb that leads to slaughter,
Being, more than lamb, God's daughter.
Acheron, as well, is blood.
But to wine run the waters
With the devils of the revels.
Fools follow after a lamb,
But God has other daughters.
These nymphs neither grow wool,
Though beautiful,
But are flesh to fly low
Where hell is heaven nearer
In bright ladies dearer;
Nor bleat and babble
To the dazzled male rabble,
Their allure is quiet and antique
And modern, being Greek.

Jews

An old enravishment of all the hearts
Of heaven may or may not have been theirs.
Their coming was too bright with candled arts
And sunny shadows to proclaim them heirs
Of any holy mystery of birth.
Hapless and unmysterious they thrive
Like flowers by themselves torn out of earth,
Martyrs and stubborn miracles alive
Upon the spiteful victory of pain.
But when their barren blossoming is full
In season some old ravishment again
Or only a perverse defiance will pull
Each proud, uprooted alien of the air
Back to a death implanted quietly
At last where every triumph of despair
Grinds dark the clouded dust of mystery.

Judgement Day

Into the home of the homeless drifted the waifs,
Wandered the wreckage of love and love's wreckers too.
Horror had emptied its kennels, life had let loose
All the unclean, unrewarded draymen of woe.
Sick nursed the sick and the hungry feasted the starved.
Men with no portion found lack to portion with lack.

Into the palace of plenty danced the provided.
Laughter had lips for itself but ears for no other.
Fortunate lovers parted in fortune's excess.
Monies were bargained for nothing, prices of humor.
Pleasure was only no-pain and pain but no-pleasure.
Harvests unhungered are never harvests at all.

This is the judgement on every soul that must die:
Either a common despair or a dreary delight.

Lines in Farewell

Where it was hard to say I said good-bye.
The stricken self in me I have abandoned
So many times, my eyes ahead to night
And death like a new soul. Farewell my mind
Of days and of a day. Rest with my name
While I give two feet over to their wind
And rush like murder among babes to where
Quiet absolves me that I ever was
Or twisted words to break out of my breath
And summon me in other mouths backward
To too much living and to less than death.
As many times it speaks, bury the spirit
In its own space of pride, and go, and fly.
It is no shame to see into the dark
Where feet outlast all memory and find
Though senseless, peace and a path.

Locomotive

Birth was the hardy drill and hammering
Not of an outward growth against a shell
Of iron split to sunlight, but the frame
Nakedly welded from the sacrifice
Of what men parted with to build me whole.
I did not waken to finished infancy
But knew my body prematurely in
The patient making and felt life driven in,
Toughened unwillingly, sucked into steam.
I had grown old before I was complete
And died with the first whistle that shrieked me done
And dead beyond decrepitude of self.
Only the tear of travel is my adventure
Into a certainty of men but not
Of me, innocent of my dangerous way
Whose guilt or gain is theirs together with
This human name I cannot answer to.

Love Was No Tether...

Love was no tether about the heart with me,
But liberated me through you.
Love was no plant trimmed to a single tip,
But spreading, partite –
I have reached out with it,
Encompassing the far dreams of its central roots.

Lawless, I broke the rule of one,
Fleeing you, fearing the lonely limit.
Ah, but the rule of many and a million,
Never to rest, never to love too little, too long,
To be thus driven....

Love was a lash upon my feet,
No tether about the heart –
Oh, that it had been this,
Meeting the various need once and forever,
And then –
Peace!

Makeshift

I stood once at the tip of the earth,
Feeling myself no longer still,
But tossed with it about the sun
In an exquisite insecurity.

Behind me
Words
And the clothes of my sobriety
And people.

Before me
The sky
Parting like a curtain
Upon the ecstacy of all the universes beyond.

Oh, who was my unknown lover, there at the edge,
Come like a cloud to me,
Too large for my beholding?

I threw back my head for him
And he loved my throat
And brushed the tips of my breasts
And caressed my whole body,
Making me giddy with the sense of myself
And of the space about me
That was my lover.

Had I perceived too much?
Had my lover wearied of me so soon?
Or were my feet too quiet,
Planted perilously on the tip,
Too safe for leaping?

For the sky dropped again before me,
Formal and final as the end of a play,
And my words came to me again
And clothes
And people
And one among them, one of all others,
Who put his arms about me

49

And paid a ceremony to my lips
And to whom I answered:
I love you.

What else could I do,
Planted at the tip of the earth,
With my blossom lifted to the sky?
What else is left?

I will get me a child,
Another to yearn at the edge,
Better beloved than myself, perhaps,
Less secure, perhaps.

On Excavating at Tell el-Amarna

The sun is a sad eye
Watching over Amarna.

Scratch the earth. Gouge all its memories:
A street, and stout jugs with their handles on their hips,
A basket and a step and roofless walls
All pleading for reality
And come again at last to consciousness
Of what they were
Or what they are supposed to be
And made themselves after a long forgetfulness.

Burrow, burrow –
One sat and worshipped here,
Another climbed these steps to –
Ask not the sun, the reminiscent sun
That is like an old woman and never will forget.

Burrow, burrow –
Ikhnaton, come up too!
The sun wants you.
You remember him, don't you?
The sun, the Aton,

Sign of Harakhte, rejoicing in the Horizon
In his name: Heat which is in Aton.

You, Ikhnaton, that were once Amenhotep,
Lonely man of Thebes, –
Lonely man of Akhetaton,
Horizon of the Aton, –
He misses you!

Come up, Ikhnaton.
The rays of the sun are his arms
That he is stretching out to you,
And on them are the hands that you have given him.
He wants to talk to you.
He has an apology to make.
He is sorry.
And he remembers how you said
That he was not the mirror of the earth
But the clear window of the God
That was mankind's divinity....

Come up, Ikhnaton.
He'd love to hear you talk again
And see the temples that you built to him
And feel your reverence warm upon himself.

Ikhnaton, Ikhnaton –
The sun is almost crying.
He never meant to burn you up like that
And make you say that you were dying of
Your enemies and that the Hittites and
The Hebrews were your friends
While he was in the sky.

Poor sun.
He's found out since then
And all his unapparent ways
Are on men's tongues
And all his radiance pinned upon a truth.
And he will never be a god or yet
The window of a god again,
And he will never be a sign

For anything but his untraveled self
And his surmised, circuitous deceit.

Come up, come up!
He's sorry that he ever told you that
He was no symbol but a god himself
And that he'd scorch your youth to a young death
If you'd make him a cresset in the sky
And not resplendent God himself.

Ikhnaton, Ikhnaton –
Come up, come up!
He promises to be a window or
A cresset or a sign or anything
You want him to if you'll come up again.

For he is but a sad eye now,
Watching forever
Over Amarna,
Over the Nile.

On Having a Poem Accepted by a Magazine

It grew diffidently in my garden,
Half-sure of its fragrance,
Wistfully designed to be a bookmark
In an unread book of
Memory and crumble like rose petals
Pressed to brittleness and
Sear with an old age that should not have been
Lived at all, however
Sweetly, redolently.

Now it goes to be a boutonnière to
Some fine gentleman all
Tidied for to-day's brief gallantries, and
I am wondering if
Some fair passing flirt will pluck my nosegay

Coyly from his coat and
Let its wilted petals shower into
An old lovers' scrapbook,
Fittingly forgotten.

Preparations for Departure

I have been with the trees all day.
I don't think they will remember what I said.
The wind came between us
And we dreamed a little on either side of it
And our dreams may have met.
I think I felt a tremor in the leaves once
While my fingers dreamed of playing them....
I have been with the trees all day,
Learning to forget.

Now I may go.
I have removed all trace of me.
Where I sat, where I walked, where I slept,
Where a corner I loved resembled me too much,
In my most private places, I have set
Something unlike me,
Something to make them strange to themselves again,
Something to make them forget.

With you, I have done none of these things,
Sure if I went out quietly enough
You would not miss me more than yesterday,
Having forgotten so long already
That a parting sign from me
Might make you remember,
Regret my going.

I have picked up
Every bit of me scattered about
And buried all of it.... somewhere.... I forget....
Over the wall!
I am going out
As somebody else!

Requital

Passed like a talisman from hand to hand,
I have increased myself with each new love
And multiplied my little thrust above
Its single impulse for the wild demand
Of every crying lover that might stand
Awaiting me to stir me with the glove
Of irresistable defiance and shove
From him this dangerous contraband.

To be repeated, echoed in each place
Where I have rested and departed whole,
Though I had left the whole of me behind, –
It was for this I quitted your embrace
And now come back to pay my numbered toll
And be as often divided in the wind.

She Pitied Me

She pitied me because my ways were smooth
And not point-peaked with pleasure.

She pitied me my body and came to soothe
Me in her hurried leisure.

She pitied me and ruefully would augur
That I should have no lover.

And now we're lying in our graves here mauger
And pitying each other.

Spirit of This Strange Age

The years he was not here – what years they were
Without him they best know, gone to some heaven
Of old familiarity that he
Had never taken the patience to think about –
We have forgotten with the kind of winds
We used to love to fly against and part
To make a little room for all of us
Where winds passed through and over. There have been
New winds, new years and this experiment
Of what may be a world, since once he came,
A stranger to make strange the previous cloak
Of habit we had worn and weathered in
The snows and summers of inheriting days
Until, converted to this mode of him,
We now go clothed in wonder and difference.

Nothing can ever be ours again, for he
Has stripped our old, ancestral shrine of its
Long faith of self-possession and availed
Him of the passing doubt of troubled youth
For what had once been young and doubting, too,
To be the god of what he'd have us say
And sing and be and do, a god too wise
To let him be believed, believed in, but
Preferring to believe in us as he
Redeemed us from our ancient gods, stranger
Of time, spirit of this strange age of his.

Tact

God sleeps all week and only wakes on Sundays.

Grind your knives.
Turn all the little wheels that make things go
And take your wickedness to walk with you.
Irreverently air your hunger and your grief
And curse the chance that gave you life.

Curse even God.
God is a sound sleeper.
He won't hear you.

Be more careful on Sundays.
God wakes on Sundays.
Sheathe your knives.
Stop the wheels.
Go virtuously dressed
In a decorous innocence.
Serve friendliness and dinners with
A Sunday generosity.
God will be gayly pleased
With larger newspapers
And comic sheets for jollity
And all his children clean from pious baths.
He'll clasp his benedictory hands and say:

"It's such a pretty place!
Fond relatives,
Starched children,
Silk mothers,
Fathers with comfortable knees,
And cunning fowls in platters
Squatting in their gravy."

Children, be good. It's Sunday.
And beggars, there's free coffee at the Mission.
Keep dresses clean. Don't quarrel.
Wear your best hat.
And let us take a walk and show dear God
How happy we all are.

God is so sensitive about his world.

We'll have to go to church
And sing some hallowed hymn
For lullaby until he falls asleep.

We can't go on like this forever.

The Ballad of the Little Old Women of Rome

The Pope is dead! And quickly then
The little old women of Rome
Come flying, flying, flying when
They hear the Pope's gone home.

A rasping flock of carrion crows,
They hunt a quarry of grace.
With hungry heads beyond their toes
They fly to see his face.

But oh, where is the thorny crown
Of him who called him Pope?
And all the little old women frown
For their inveigled hope.

But oh, where are the hammered feet
Of him who held their faith?
They sought a Christ and only greet
The body of a wraith.

The little old women turn away,
The little old women of Rome.
And they will wait till Judgement Day
For a pope to take them home.

The Basket

On my maiden arm swinging
In and out of my shadow
It made its own song,
Its own day and night.

The fruits are fewer now.
There is a bottom in the burden.
Light leaks out of the weave,
The straw trembles to a breath,
Too smooth to rustle, and rarely

The fruits are fated, in this late falling,
To be suspicious, pelt me.

So no more to market
My merry basket.
Next season drop my bones in it,
Enlist a ghost to bear the harvest
In and out of my shadow
Up and down death
For its own song,
Its own day and night.

The Carnival

How can a carnival be wearier than a plain day?
But only a tin crown and no chosen queen is left over,
And the crumpled festivities slide in the wind, crinkle away.
Go home, put the pennies back, go home.
Be less inquisitive among the wreckage than disdainful.
Disgust without previous delight is tearless.
The split fruit of sorrow makes a life and death;
And afterwards, in the eternal famine,
Tinkles the echo of a carnival that hissed the first fire long ago.
Life is too late by death, death is too late by life.
Who is a falconer of joy is a missing man
Among the living and a dead man among the dead.
Go home.

The Cheat

Magnificent moment of my birth –
Round copper in my hand I held you,
Time-treasure.
I might buy anything with you.

Irrevocable mistake –
I bought from time another moment with you,
Just ahead, brighter-seeming;
This was the thing to do, Time said.
But thinner, dimmer, my new treasure –
I have been bargaining ever since with Time,
Coin for deceptive coin,
Till I have little left to buy me anything.

On, on!
Can I not buy with what I have
That old magnificent moment of my birth?
On, on!
Too late, too late,
Too costly now,
Too cheaply sold,
Only enough to buy the moment beyond,
Loss upon loss till at the end
I shall have but enough for buying death
That I can get for nothing any day.

Magnificent moment of my birth –
How Time has profited,
Little by little despoiling
That first abundance of mine,
Dealing me slowly death in turn,
Hoarding her own forever!

The Crime of John Eldridge Katell

In our town there was none so public-spirited
As John Eldridge Katell. He'd work all day at sums
In the Town Hall recording all the born and dead
As if he thought a divine revelation comes

From adding and subtracting heads, as if he thought
That truth was a totality. He had a craze
For marking birth a minus, death a plus and life a naught.
We laughed at what we called his queer recorder ways.

We laughed because we did not understand how he
Was Malthus-mad and would have made the unasked gift
Of life a meager measure of economy,
And wept for every birth and thought that death would lift

The mortal curse of life that is too much with us.
He smiled at funerals and visited the sick.
Even when all his children died, he made no fuss.
We fondly ranked him with the brave and called him Stoic.

We never knew what made him shoot ten Christian men.
And John Eldridge Katell lies twelve years in his sod.
We never understood devout John Eldridge when
He shrieked out his last words: For Malthus and for God.

Since that perplexed and all too unforgotten time
A dozen weary wonder-tangled words have fled.
But yet our town has never understood the crime
Of John Eldridge Katell the public-spirited.

The Ghoul

Life is death.
Living is dying.
There are teeth in the flesh
And the meat is not merry
And the mouth is not hungry
And the wasteful ghoul is no ascetic,
Leaves too much on the bone
For the worms and the weather to clear away.

The ghoul of the true grave
Is slave to no appetite,
But crunches at a command,
The same command that fattens us.

Oh miserable banquet.
The unknown jaw chews regularly at us
To a music we love,

And the vanity of tasting good
Sweetens us,
And the wine that washes us down
The gullet of a sober ghoul
Stirs a drunkenness in us
That makes us die twice
Who can only be eaten once.

The Judge

Flesh finding two lonely lives
Each side of it,
Torn up between the two –
Oh three,
Mute a little while in single harmony
Where each unrecognizable
Sings quietly, sleeps,
While death listening decides
Which shall wake....

The Kiss

My mite of love buried away
Behind my loveless pauper glance,
My cup scraped of the sticky sweet
My strict mouth will not countenance
But that beneath my tongue can stay
Some roving pirate kiss to greet –

How can I call the kiss and keep
My lips unbroken here for it
And cry my love aloud to lure
Love to my singing infinite
This dying voice would sing impure?

I can but wait and be the thing
I must if I would please the heart
That yet because I am like this,
Too surely hidden and apart,
As it would have me, cannot bring,
Deliverance and the brave kiss.

The Lost Isle

Death flew with me,
A bird of no alighting place,
Wingless, riveted upon the air,
Death, the carrier between nothing and nothing.

Death dropped me by mistake,
Narrowly through the air's thin morass,
Light and sure as a thought I fell
Into the lost isle of the living
(Death cried after,
Death promised to come back himself
For me and all the rest, some time).

Not alone, I. Death had been careless.
We were many together.
Life was an unintended shower
Watering the garden isle where we had planted
Slips of a sempiternal bloom,
Should Death ever remember,
Should Death ever come back to gather us
(Or, if Death forgot,
Yet to be fair in field,
Full in harvest for our own sake).

Seed for seed, age for age,
That death might find us as we had been,
Unwearied, waiting afresh,
We have invented birth,
We have invented a dying of our own,
Calling patience time,
Committing us to these till Death comes.

Death has grown careful, never dropping,
Seeing perhaps, how many we have made ourselves already.
Does Death fly at all now?
What have we done to Death,
Inventing dying?

Pledged, perpetual,
Serving our own thrall
And so involved in dying,
We can't escape to find what has happened to Death –
Is there no way?
We might be happy here on this lost isle forever.
Is there no way to circumvent dying?
But if we found a way,
Death might be reawakened, reminded,
Death might come for us.

Dying, lost:
At least we have found a way
To circumvent Death.
We have invented dying.
Why should Death trouble,
Why should Death come?

The Masterpiece of Lope Juan

In Filamona people never had
Done anything but watch Lope grow old.
When he was young he moved them to a wonder
For what he did not do. He was no child
To babble in a child's wise way of things
That elders never see or if they do
See with an unaware indifference,
As one will scarcely look up at the sky,
Knowing how it is there perpetually
Because it always has been. Lope Juan,
They said, was never known to ask a question.
And yet through an impenetrable sense

That was as unaccountable to them
As if it were a dream – for both had been
As little willed – they did not call him dolt,
Devining somehow that his silence was
A greater questioning than might have been
The greatest reckoning of idle *why's*
Sweetly to overflow the brimming pride
Of one enamored mother. And there was
Another hitherto uncounted sense
That taught them that he had been answered by
A larger wisdom. For they seemed to see
How much the lesson of one day's communing
With the earth's unimagined little things,
A moment's brief amazement for a sunset,
Could give him and respected it beyond
What all of them together might have taught
That boy within a hundred laden years.
By that same understanding, such a one
That's only known to those who briefly read
The burden of a lifetime in a line
Mysteriously wrought of all the strength
Of handclasps indurately given, – if there
Indeed are such – they also vaguely knew
When he had taken all that one might take
From sunsets and the little things of earth
Without encountering godliness, enough
To leave him with a tongue to speak
To his own kind with a magnificence
That barely overflowed the little measure
Of their discrimination, but enough
Yet to anoint them with its wizardry,
To baffle them to praise the greater part
They could not understand and venerate
In awed incomprehensibility.
And they could truly say in later years
When pilgrims came to touch adoringly
Whatever he had touched and stroke the bed
He died upon and wonder at his palette
Devoutly, as if there might be some trace
Of genius to be disentangled from
The riotous web all knit with glory there,
That they had always proudly realized

The kind of man he was. They gently vied
In reminiscences, sure that there were
No others but themselves to represent
In wistful recollection his strange ways
Of doing little ordinary things
In an unwonted wise, how he was gentle
And yet had never given evidence
Of gentleness, how his unparted lips
Were silent with more kindnesses than could
Have been the message of benevolence.
For Filamona had been his Ravenna
As it had been his Florence, and it shared
Its memories as jealously with others
As if all that were left of Lope Juan
Were thin remembrances of what he'd been
And not the testament of what he'd done,
As if they really thought that he had lived
More faithfully in time than in his colors –
Not that they loved their recollections more
Than his own works, but that they grimly felt
How covetously had his art craved him
And what a generous giver he had been,
Yielding to each surrender of himself
That he himself desired insatiably
As if it were another one that lay
Impaled in paint upon his canvases.
And there was no one in that little town
That had grown smaller yet from all its years
Of huddling round the story of one man,
As you will find a forest closely brooding
Over its silences, no one more shaped
By the endearments of proximity
To tell the tale of Lope Juan than Diego,
His servant, if it could be said at all
That Lope ever needed anything
Beyond his palette's nurture, though that fed
The greater half of him that was not called
Himself, and left the hunger of the other
To be a holocaust for all the rest.

So Diego gravely spat upon the ground
And cleared his throat as if to rid himself

Of anything that might defile the tale
Of Lope Juan and tightly stroked his head
As if to titillate his unbent thought
To a brisk pageant of the sober days
That Lope Juan had gently lived with him.

"We knew when he had come to speak, and yet
We were all stretched upon our expectation
As you might dangle on a window-sill
To see around the corner. And no matter
That we had never understood his work.
It was enough for us that he had painted.
I still can see it hanging there, that frame
That barely kept the color tongues within
From leaping out in an enlivened flame;
And I have always thanked the Lord that Juan
Was never one to paint upon the air,
For had he been, then lying on his back
Upon the earth as if the unlimned sky
Were some colossal Vatican, who knows
What divine world of aching glory he
Had painted on the canvas of the clouds,
What futile terrors to surpass the stars,
The trivial stars, and what magnificence
To emulate preposterously the brood
Of dainty, mawkish pastels feebly bred
By that old sentimental hand the sun
In an unchaste old age. And yet would he
For such Promethean temerity
Have suffered more than all he slowly did
In his long dying, knowing well himself,
As well as all the rest of us, how much
Of his short life he gave to every picture
He painted, just enough to dower it
With an eternity of fame? And so
We came to watch his works with a strange hate
For every beauty he encompassed there
With an insidious stroke that did not tell
From what far depths they rose to entity;
And rested wantonly upon his easel,
Thus lewd for the abandon of his life
In moments subtly woven to a cloak

66

For their ambitious nudity – not that
I mean to say he lived his ardent life
Exhaustively in time, but rather that
Time seemed to be the measure of what he gave
For his art's sake, so that it can be said
That he lived rather in all else but time.
Take that first painting I was speaking of
And called the 'Corpse', significantly called,
As if he knew that something of himself
Was buried there beyond recapturing.
They came and dexterously fingered it
With adept glances shrewdly aimed to see
The crucifix that was a skeleton
For all his magic to be draped upon,
And they were men to read the symbol wisely.
'A genius here.' 'A masterpiece!' And then,
'There is a *soupçon* of Velasquez here.'
Well, so it went, he writing his own threne
In polychromic verse for critics' words
To trickle the dull shadows of their praise
Upon.
          He scarcely seemed to know at all
If they had spoken, and listened all the less
To his old mother when she begged of him
To paint no more. 'It's killing you, my son.'
But he would pat her then abstractedly
Upon the back as if she'd gently said
In her caressing diffidence, 'My son,
What a fine day we have!' For Lope knew
As well as all of us how much his fate
Was as inevitable as the weather.

"Well, after he had finished his 'La Pena',
We said who knew him: Lope Juan has not
The pigment in him for another picture,
Be it the smallest, frailest miniature
Of what is smallest in our little town.
Nor was 'La Pena' thought the least of all
That he had painted, for those same critics
Had wrung cups of dry-mouthed and dour delight
From it and yet the canvas was somehow
Miraculously whole, but rather then

67

It was so full of him that we sat down
To watch the last of him as if he was
The lingering last act of some old play
We'd seen a score of times before, that had
Come querulously back to make its bow
And shake hands with the audience perhaps
As would some petted drama of De Vega's.
But we were wrong to think that his last act
Would be the idle drawing of a curtain
On what had been already finely done.
Oh, you will say, I know: 'Come, now, my friend,
Don't sentimentalize. Now, I suppose,
You'll tell me that he fell in love and that
His love he deemed his greatest work of all
Because it took the rest and most and last
Of him for its fulfillment.' Well, perhaps
That's near the truth, but only as one might
Address a star in deference to the moon
Or choose some simpler beauty to approach
A greater. In a sense you're blindly right.
He fell in love and in it came to find
His greatest work. You've heard of 'Finita'
Or seen it somewhere? – just an old woman
Made to fit sharply in a frame – his best,
They say, and say not knowing why, as if
They had in some unseeing way devined
Its essence. Who Finita was? And well
You do to ask. Ah, no, there is no story
Of an old woman whom he loved, for she
Was Fina, or Finita, as he loved
To call her, a caress for the soft scarf
That floated on her shoulders, and her face
A slender marvel for her fringing hair.
But he would say: 'Finita, I am old
And dying, my Finita. Is there not
Young Pedro with a vigor for your youth?'
And little Fina would just laugh and say:
'Well then, my master, I will run like this
And this and catch up with you to be old
And dying too like you.' And then she'd run
Around the room until poor Lope Juan
Would laugh for grief and hold Finita close,

Until one day, with a strange humor come
To quiver resolutely in his eyes,
He took her hands and said: 'You mean it then
That you would die with me if you could help?'
'Why, surely, Lope Juan, and are you one
To ask?' He kissed her then as coldly as
A mother and made her sit down in a chair
And said that he would paint a picture, such
A one as never had been painted yet,
And that she must sit very still and smile
Directly at him while he painted her
And never move and never ask to see
What thing it was he made till it was done.
Four days and nights I waited there on them,
Yet scarcely waited, for Finita ate
As little as himself, but smiled as if
She would have desperately wrought
Some gentleness in his cruel magic there.
When the fifth morning came to greet his task,
Then Lope Juan took Fina by the hand
And tucked the portrait underneath his arm
And sent me quickly through the town to cry
That Lope Juan would presently arrive
Upon the marketplace to show his last
And greatest work. He set the picture down
With an old man's precision and then placed
Finita opposite it. 'Kind friends,' he said –
Oh, he was very gay that day – 'Behold,
Good gentlemen, my masterpiece!' The veil
Was gently drawn. There was no sign to speak
His meaning yet, for all they saw at first
Was an old woman sharply bent within
A frame. But gradually those who stood
A little nearer than the rest began
To cry: 'Why, there is something strange in this!
That hag there wears Finita's eyes and all
That our Finita is, grown old. Good God,
There is some devil's meddling here!' Who knows
Whose hand it was? Finita looked at it
For one protracted moment and then died
As if the old age of that hag had come
Upon herself. Some say she smiled and cried:

'Together now my Lope!' But there have
Been many legends of that day to curl
Themselves around it like the smoke around
Some furtively inviolable fire.
And what of him? Well, why should there be more,
Since he had done his last and greatest work?
He lived just long enough to prove that when
He feebly died he had always been dead
Inexorably since that dim old day
When his last step of talent had climbed up
To its expectant consummation. And
That picture? Someone found it there and paid
Its price to Pedro, to whom it had been willed.
He spluttered over it and said it would
Become the greatest yet of all of them –
A transcendental study of old age,
A gage to fame, a priceless heritage
To art, and other things. He came to me
And asked me if I knew what it was called.
I wryly said: 'The End of Lope Juan.'
But such a worry came to twist his face
That, as one asks forgiveness for a smile
Untimely shaped, I deprecatingly
Dismissed my jest and simply told him with
A hidden, unsuspected significance
That Lope Juan had called her 'Finita'.

"Well, that is all. I hope it can't be said
I've sentimentalized. No tears, no ghosts,
Unless you should perhaps yourself some day
Go shadow-monging in the Gallery
And see what youth may lie behind old bones
Bent sharply to the limits of a frame."

Postscript

We never will admit in Filamona
That Master Lope Juan created beauty.
We will agree that it is there upon
His canvases. But you have not our eyes
To see the grace that has supinely fled

70

From every tree and face that Lope Juan
Ever beguiled to faithlessness to its
Own inwrought image. For he was a blight
To beauty, and when he passed, it was
As if Medusa and not he had passed,
As if what he had painted was afraid
To find its rival in its model. But
In Filamona we have learned to love
Our poverty, knowing how brilliantly
Lope emblazoned the treasures he had stolen.

The Music Teacher

There was a time, I've heard, when she could play
With something like a fierceness to arouse
A quiet joy in those who loved her way
Of flinging torture in a wild carouse
Of beauty grown articulate. The sun
Gave no more madly than did she, for when
She loudly flayed the silence, she was one
To quicken all the dormant things in men
That wake to understanding at a touch
From one small finger sentiently attuned
To strike a long unsounded note. One such
Had heard her until he was starkly pruned
Of everything that did not bear some fruit
Of her own fostering. Then for a year
She played on him until she came to suit
The measure to his mood. She could not hear
The music. It was as if she had created
Something too large for hearing. She had a fear
That almost fathomed how much she was hated.
And once she saw half-leaping from his eyes
The hate that she had only guessed. It came
A stifled echo from which she could devise
The larger rhythm, as sparks mount to a flame,
As one remembered chord may subtly build
An old and long forgotten melody.
And now it was as if she'd really willed

To play that tune. She played more savagely
Than she had ever played. He was a sky,
She said, a slate-gray sky, and she would not
Be dimmed by him, but rend him till he'd cry
For night, and that her touch would be so hot
That he would cry for coolness. And he cried
For both. She played a dirge *scherzo* for token
Until both came together. And so he died
Only when she had left no string unbroken.

She is a tidy widow now, not pretty,
But with something like a vigorous content
For what has been superbly done. Not pity
Sends her pupils, but a presentiment
Of what she has to teach. They seem to see
The agony-fraught notes that they can learn
From her, and how to find a cruelty
In all the gentleness of a nocturn.
She's suffered little maidens to come to her
And built them to a stern, envenomed race,
One that can wield a strain to wound and stir
A melody to malice in her place.

The New Atlas

An underdog, well-grounded at the bottom
And agile for all that for balancing
A pyramid turned upside down on me
And spinning buoyantly upon my back.
Who else was there for me to free poor Atlas?

They tell me that it is an evil thing
That I have no ambition in me to scale
Their wheeling pyramid and see myself
How giddily ecstatic one may grow
From corybantic spinning the air.

72

I am a conscientious beast to be
Ridden by such a boisterous company,
And yet were I less faithful, who would be
Another patient mountain for all their
Imponderability to rest upon?

And I should not care to be otherwise,
For some day, from much whirling on my back,
They will become deliriously light
And hover on me airily as clouds.

May I be as a mountain to them then.

The Scourge

I am the woman of no tears.
I am the woman of no smiles.
The world marches upon me,
An army bannered with lights.
There is one who leads them
And his plume is a torch
And my heart is a cold crisp cinder,
Small trophy to an enemy.
I have cut the string and thrown it behind me
That it may be recognized for what it is,
A cold crisp cinder,
That it may no longer be called the thing it is not.

Oh, the world marches upon me,
An army bannered with lights.
Yet I shall cry war upon them,

Though all that were my people
Have lanterned their spears with light against me,
Though their songs be hot on their tongues,
Though they tear out their tongues for arrows.

"Burn bright,
Battle light,
Burn white,
Bone reaching,
Bone bleaching!"

(These are the things their tongues cry out to me.)

"She has said,
The woman of no tears,
The woman of no smiles,
        'The world is too bright.
        Day dazzles
        With the world's
        Uncountable faces.

        'The world is too bright.
        Put the sun out.
        The world is too many.
        Let death darken the world's uncountable faces
        Beyond seeing.
        The world is too bright.
        Day dazzles.
        Put the sun out.
        Day dims to night.
        Night is not dim enough.
        Night glimmers and flickers.
        Death shines not at all.

        'The world is too bright.
        The world is too loud
        With the sounds
        Of the world's uncountable faces.
        Anger plots behind teeth.
        Hate is a miser mumbling in throats.
        Joy is a castanet upon the lips.

        'Sorrow is a wheel upon the forehead.
        Pain comes crying out of the eyes.
        Peace whispers behind the ears.
        Love sings in the hair.
        The world is too loud.

74

The world is not still enough.
Sleep mutters and only muffles her voices.
Death says nothing at all.'

"This is the song of the woman of no tears.
This is the song of the woman of no smiles.
She has made doors of her eyes.
She has made locks of her ears,
Keeping a hostile solitude,
Chanting this prayer:

     'The world's uncountable faces bloom and scatter
     And return in their seeds again.
     Death, will you make one final gathering,
     Taking me last of all
     That I may have a second's knowing of
     What I am like alone?'

This is the prayer of the woman of no tears.
This is the prayer of the woman of no smiles,
Fury of ill hope,
Friend of the silence that will breathe again,
The enemy.

"Burn bright,
Battle light,
Burn white,
Bone reaching,
Bone bleaching!"

The world has marched upon me,
An army bannered with lights.
Victory is a multitude.
Defeat is an exile,
Leaning far out upon the edge of all things.

I have climbed the Peak of the Last Look Backward,
Pared to a pencil-point,
Dotting the sky with new stars,
Sharpened beneath me,
Brief parting poignancy.

The world and I are at peace again
For one last moment's forever.
Hushed are the world's uncountable faces
Morning will find them once more loud and bright,
Happily unreviled,
Let them rest,
Let them rest.
I would not have them witness
To my first swift leap
Upon that single path of darkness
Where I must ultimately find
What I am like alone.

The Sin

That nun
Needs no sheath of sombreness
Against what lies beyond the gate.
There may be many sinful folds
In a cloak of chastity.

The bars
Of the cloister gardens
Are not made for flaying reverence.
And her passion
Is not unconscionably more than that.
Though who knows
What may be hidden
Underneath that gown?

The stone
That lines the cloister courtyard
Plays a cold accompaniment to pious heels.
She walks there
To swish the hem of her gown
Ecstatically against it.
And for this luxury
The sensuous courtyard
Makes her an award of secrecy.

The bars
And the stones.
She is wise to choose such confidants
Adamant like herself.
Do not forget the folds of her gown,
Sinuously inscrutable
And black only for piety.

One Other
Who hangs above her bed
Knows the burden of her beads.
There was no one to say
It was wrong to hang it there.

For Him
There are
No sinuously inscrutable folds.

At night
She takes off the blackness of her chastity
And bares the whiteness of her sin.

The Thief

He is young and ugly.
He has eyes, soft as an ox's,
And he writes of the Gods and Women.

He is wrinkled and stuttering.
He is ashamed, like a mongrel,
And he sings me songs on the road.

Where is his body,
Where is his white body,
Proud with poems,
Tall with songs?

You somewhere with the slinking soul,
You somewhere with the tall proud body,
Thief, stand in the light.

The Torch

My little house is all unlit at night.
Will ever there be one to bear a light
Before me through each room and put to sleep
A memory that I shall sadly keep
Unwakened until on another night
Another comes, bearing his gallant light
Before me that old memories may leap
To life and a young love be put to sleep?

They Pass Each Other in the Dance...

They pass each other in the dance but twice:
Children and mothers, mothers merry-footed
And children swaddled in their babyhood,
Awkward for galloping and slow, unseeing
And tardy for rapidity, missing
The moment's clasp and parting. But mothers wait.
But mothers pause and wait, indulgent, impatient.

They pass each other in the dance but twice:
Children and mothers, children spirited
For brevity, not loving passings, because
They pause and smile and weep and linger, giving
The dance a rest and time for tired return;
And mothers, finding dances cruel because
They fleet, forgetting, and leave no slow repose
For those who would be glad for a small sadness
And a minute device of parting in passing.
Yet children wait a little, indulgent, impatient.

The mothers halt, the dance goes on beyond,
Bearing the children to a further place.
Still and asunder, both wait another passing.
But endless pausing knows no quiet approach.
They pass each other only in the dance.
They pass each other in the dance but twice.

To Another

Whom I have understood even less than any,
Who did not love me but was only loyal
But loyal so little it seemed only love.
He made too much of me, denied himself
Too utterly, offered the comfort of
A lovable excess of adoration,
Forgot he came to me upon a sorrow
Like the repentance of a storm in sun,
But no new day. Was it without a thought
He stopped the act of worship and stood up,
Choked off the heaven he had seen in me
Because it fell too close about his earth?
Or did he, frightened with so much success,
Flee from my gratitude and the disgrace
Of having without love consoled a woman?

To B.S.B.
(In Memoriam)

I

He came too sweetly to be strong,
He came too lightly to stay for long.
A sea lasts back to its first lake.
A hill travels from the heart of the earth
To its most single tree.
A man wears out wearily
With life. Many ruins make the ruin
Entire of an enduring flesh or stone.
A child needs death alone
To end the more than life
In the less than flesh.

II

A moody wind blew him across
A canyon to a mother like a forest.
She was an early shelter
Where he must learn to wander
And be soon safely lost of her
Among the wastrels of the destinate storm.
Her roots feared, denied him outwardness.
Her leaves relented, taught him too much light,
Revealed him more of the sky
Than of the world root-tumbled out of sight.
The child asked why, wished for the earthly difference,
And went, and won it
When the snow came
And the wood missed just so much
In the numb shadow of a leaflessness.

III

Afterwards unaware the winter lakes,
The snowy meadows mused on him
Unnoticeably as a hundred years
Will owe one sadness to forgetting him
So lovingly.
Like a sunlit mote upon the dark scene
He fluttered and fled.
The darkness is new now after him.
In every child it takes, death denies a light,
Lights the spell of an unseen
Where the dead child lives
Until the living child dies.
Listen, mothers of ghosts,
Let your hearts see not too well,
Too tenebrously,
But be blind with grief,
Sightless of the living grave,
As the winter lakes, as the snowy meadows,
Freeze over for a hundred years,
Forget through loving.

To One About to Become My Friend

Stand off!

I am stone.
    You must tear your flesh to excavate my heart.

I am storm.
    None can rest with me.

I am mountain.
    Toil to the top, be there a solitary.

I am ice.
    You must be frozen that I be melted.

I am sea.
    I would not give you up again.

If this frightens you,
Stand off! Stand off!

Yet, would you be my friend,
I should be none of these to you.

Tocsin

Where are the winnings of the war
Between hot and cold?
Burn your fingers on my fire,
Freeze my heart cold
Against the faint
Breast of restraint.

Love is no prize
Where meek manoeuvres equalize
With battle furious.
Kill me or keep me slave

Or else be amorously mine.
Peace is luxurious
For all but the brave.
Yet, even cowards learn to pine
For love, up from the grave.

Too Happy I

Too happy I,
Too happy I –
    Sufficient world
    Of self and sky –
My lips enchanted
With merry-berries' winey dew,
    Too sweetly fed,
    Too sweetly fed,
Fatten me now,
Fatten me now on sorrow's bread
    That I may die,
    Having starved too long.

Traitor

Good that my eyes in going
Go not as blind but dead,

That death is no defect
Of body, but something else.

Failure, my flesh, is life.
Failing, you cannot fail again

Unless this heart alone
Triumphing in love that has outlasted it
Betray me over and over eternally.

Trifle

What meanings constitute myself?
Trifle of truth,
How many indispensable trifles of me
Subscribe to my impression of totality?

If, then, you find me not partial,
But piece by piece the crescent sum of beauty,
Life may be but one more exquisite detail
Of an ageless art,
The flattering finish of time
That flashes the fair aggregate of ever
Upon the screen of a minute;

And truth, since there are so many different others,
Time's paltry and accurate deductions
From the careless space of beauty
That make me and all of us,
Since every meaning is entire and fair,
Amount to life,
A mere detail.

Truth

We keep looking for Truth.
Truth is afraid of being caught.
Books are bird-cages.
Truth is no canary
To nibble patiently at words
And die when they're all eaten up.

Truth would not like
To live in people's heads or hearts or throats.
Don't try to find her there.

Truth is no dryad to be punished in a tree.
Truth is no naiad.
Truth would be surely drowned in a spring.

Don't worry the earth.
Truth leaves no footprints.
Don't listen
Before silence has set with the moon.
Truth makes no noise.
Don't follow the light
That follows the sun
That follows the night.
Truth dances beyond the light
And the sun
And the night.
Truth can't be seen.

Let curiosity stay at home.
It may get lost.
(Truth has strange haunts.)
If stealth wears shoes
It grows up to imprudence.

Leave truth alone.
Truth can't be caught.
I think Truth doesn't live at all because
She'd have to be afraid of dying, then.

Unforfeited

They hate me in the town where I live.
They say that I have not a thing to give.
They like old evil Martin who is poor
And even in a meager way impure
As any one who drags his memories
Behind him like the marks of some disease,
They like him well because then they can quarrel
And always bring in Martin for a moral,
As History and all its tale of strife
Becomes a door-mat for our present life.
They like Anne Hepzibah Carew because
She's weak in love. They like her for the flaws
They find in her, and sitting on their porches,

They talk about her sins and thrust the torches
Of their tongues in her wounds. So now I know
Just why through all the town they hate me so.
I sit behind closed blinds and never look
At them. They say my face is like a book
In an old monastery, tightly chained
Unto myself. It's true I have disdained
All their attempts to read me. I am written
In strange tongues; if they read, they would be smitten
With fear of me much worse than their dislike.
For they do not know how I am a dike
Against their greediness, and if they guessed
How much I hated them, they'd have me blessed
Nightly on all the porches on Jackson Street.
They're folk to whom a gift of hate is sweet.
I'd rather slowly die behind my blind
Than let them know how much I hate their kind.

Wrappers

How many neat brown packages there are
That never are untied. To think that if
Your fingers had been imperceptibly
Less deft, I might be yet a prim parcel
Bristling in manila. And now you say:
"But how could all of you have ever been
So tightly rolled to fit into that case,
As if there were not room enough outside?"
See, dear, I am as sweetly serious
As a sad child that is subtly afraid
Of speaking unattended, and perhaps
You'll think me silly as himself for all
My wistful faith in promises. But say!
Some day when I have grown too raveled here
For you outside my wrapping, then go seek
My tegument on an old shelf where you
Have stored in housewifely frugality
A hundred casings like my own, and please
Be good enough to iron every crease

That you once made unwrapping me, my dear,
When it was reft in reckless eagerness
For what was tucked inside. You'll be surprised
To find how wizened I can grow for crumpling.
Be deft to swaddle me as you were once
As nimble to dismantle me. And leave
Me tidily upon your doorstep then
All wrapped and tied demurely – for another.

II

Boy with Violets

The bouquet in his hands –
Has he forgotten it?
The same he set out with,
Violets bud wilted,
Die shriveled,
These have paused somewhere,
Called in their season,
Gasped against hope
In the crush of his palm,
In the tight gloom learning
Love is nothing with the violets
Until a girl unite them
At her girdle nervously
Under her slight bosom.

For Rebecca West
(On Reading The Judge)

With what compassionate solicitude
Your book is made, Rebecca West. Whatever
Makes men and women must be so impelled.
If it be God, then God must take such trouble
As yours to put small bones and flesh together
Between a birth and death, composed with life,
God's genius, as you take words into your hands,
Crushing them finely to a body flesh
Until I cry with pain that skin should seem
So soft to touch and still not move between
A birth and death, but be a written thing
Between two covers – yet more than written thing.
Perhaps your genius is a little like God's.

Oh strange and beautiful necessity
Of God and you. I think I like yours best,
For God is slow and difficult as if
Care hesitated so from over-practice,
While you are somehow slow and yet more swift

Than God, hurrying the hand that rests to lift,
Dropping the lifted hand before it tires.
God puts his pottered people together with patience,
But now I know that patience may have wings.

Life is no different at all from this.
Though we can only touch the present page,
The book is done, we are but slow in reading.
And yet, because art is complete at once,
Being more brief to see, lasting forever,
While life is piece-meal measured, thus pledged to time,
So that it dies, don't fear I'll read the end
Before the rest, as if I'd make myself
The oracle of what's already done.
But I shall meet it minute by minute as
A life is lived, watching the glass to see
Each casual grain retire into the mass
And rise again, serried importantly
Among the others; and learn your people like
A lesson, day by day, till memory
Would ache not to be able to remember
What they were like; and give my faith to you
For having impaled such life on art and even
Permitted me to make the hurt all mine;
And then, because of what I am, touch art
With time and give it death upon the cover
And bury it in anguish in my heart....

If I could come and watch you make a book,
Some day, unseen, Rebecca West, I think
It would be like my watching God, a little.

Lovely My Flesh . . .

Lovely my flesh but extravagance rash –
Waster of beauty, the thriftiest dash
Spattered upon me were blessing enough
To redeem this stuff.

Flesh is the dark tabernacle's rimed glass
Frosted for no earthly sunbeam to pass.
Beauty anointing and melting the pane
With your warm, spring rain:

Only a drop of your heavenly dew
Surely would let heaven's light travel through.
Pamper not flesh you must quickly forsake,
That was made but to break.

Mama to Maria

Step out, Maria, and let Mars
Admire your gown
And all the foreign stars
That have moved down
Into our neighborhood.

A little lower at the neck:
Toy with your lace.
Remove one small invisible speck
And tilt your face
The way a woman should

Who wants a husband sworn by June.
If Mars is pink
And likely we shall have a moon,
I'm bound to think
The young man three doors down
Will also be polite
To newcomers in town
On such a night.

Melinda Pours

Teacups tinkle china nectar
Blessed bloodless by the Rector.
Aunt Melinda, is it right
Always to be this polite?
Can't I hiss beneath my breath
Some impertinence to death?

She determines destiny
With unspilled and perfect tea.
Now and then, appearing kinder,
She dispenses a reminder
With a soaked improper leaf:
Drinking is the soul's belief
Of a mouth that does not matter
If it only writhe and chatter
Feebly out the secret price
Of a draught of paradise.

Eyes too water-lily cream,
Elm-like tall that does not seem
Woman-like but queerly fine
For a human kin of mine.

Men and the Hymn

Swish the silent silk away.
Song is the vision under the veil
For who dare see and sing
The irresistable hymn
Of single eloquence.

Or let the still curtain hang and fray
Until a ragged litany peers
Shivering like a winter sun through snow,
And holy in your coward heart
Dies a divided harmony
Too brave.

Notwithstanding Love

I shall be always just as dark as this.
There will be no change, never a change,
Nothing to show –
I need not name the thing.

How quickly the flashes strike me and then go,
Claw my covered face, hurl cutlasses
Into my heart –
But I am shaded well.

The wounds are private matters and my own.
Multiply the night in me, oh sun,
Save for the tapers of the pain
That I alone can tell.

The last day that I am, then,
Shall be no brighter than the next,
Notwithstanding love
And all the other flames
That have fattened here.

Of Stone Is My Strong Heart

Of stone is my strong heart,
Weathered into my breast, and stern.
I prayed for fire.
Of what avail is kindling that cannot burn?
I prayed for rain.

Rain fell and cool claimed cool
In the chaste distant touch.
It is not meet
That what is stone from being soil too much
Should melt for love.

Yet, if I cannot bear a seed
Or hold a heartful up again,
The hidden spring
Of my stark self-reserve can give the rain,
Or you, to drink.

Orbits

Her first devised intention was a jest,
And old Carlotto smiled on it, as if
It were some serious young pondering
And not a canny pleasantry too bold
For his solemnity. She said: "Old man,
Do you know that I think that people all
Grow old because they are too kind? For I
Have watched the stars and skies and things that last.
I know the sun has never been aware
Of anything. The distant wind is an
Indifferent adventurer that blows
His indiscriminate breezes with a far
And timeless unconcern for timeful things,
And rocks are an eternal cruelty.
Whatever does not die is ruthless for
Its long and endless purposes and has
Its own immortal orbit that must not
Be left for anything. What beauty and
Fair winds may be are yet ungenerous
Fortuities. And I am sure that each
Of us, Carlotto, has his own assigned
Uncharitable orbit in forever.

You must have left it long ago to be
So old, so kind. But I am young and have
Not learned an elderly benevolence.
Carlotto! See! I will be like the sky,
As lovely, as regardless and as cruel."

He shook his head and said: "How wise you are!
And yet I'm frightened by the many things
You do not know and may not ever learn.
And you would laugh at me if I should say
I loved my finite perpendicular
That lifts and soars and soaring never turns
Upon old ways, beyond the largest course
That must return and going, come again
In tired, slow perpetuity." She laughed
At him and cried: "Poor man, you've grown too old.
It's time you died." Carlotto grieved and died.
"He died too soon," she said and laughed again.
"His latest kindness was myself."

                                   And now
She was indifferent as the air and years
Were birds that rested imperceptibly
On her and lightly passed and left no trace.
If she was fair, she knew it not. And she
Was yet more unaware of the distress
She wrought than of the joy, and people knew
They could not blame her, for she only was
And did not live at all,

                          until one day
She halted in her circumambient way
With resolute mortality and said
She thought she had encompassed everything,
And yet she had not once seen old Carlotto
Who had begun to soar so long ago.
Then she unbent her deathless orb and vowed
She would grow wonderfully old and be
Unconquerably kind until she'd die
Victoriously and catch up with her old
And kind and rectilinear Carlotto.

Perinot Olad

Perinot Olad, of such tongue
And translating trickery,
He could tell for the whole world,
Was deprecated poet not for his tongue
But the soul in his soft flesh fumblingly.

He had told for all but three million ten
And some flabby Eskimos and slippery Chinese
And wept over and over faithfully:
"There is no death but in this ignorance of it."
When suddenly he stumbled over his confession to his knees,

Found himself dead and disappointed
Together with three million ten, all his clients,
Dead, damn, and they knew it.
The knowledge was born of the ignorance.
They cursed him for opposing poetry to science.

Science might have disciplined them into the universe
And oblivion. It could surely have done no worse
Than Perinot Olad born preaching like an old man
And singing, singing himself young, young until now
He seemed unsedately dead and a babe.

As a babe he babbled the charm a shade
Revised for the vague requirements of the occasion:
"There is no death but in this knowledge of it."
They were delighted with the exorcism,
Retained him as priest against the next metamorphosis.

But by this time Perinot Olad was nearly full infant
Impending under his new mother's breast triumphant,
Immortally mortal to inspire the three million ten tripled:
"There is no death but in this ignorance of it."
Now all were content in this quibble, the living to
    be dead, alive, the dead to be alive, dead.

Perspective

Now I have wearied of the intimate range
Who never raised my eyes to reach a place
I might not dream or see without some change
Of stunted vision, but I loved the close embrace
Of native idols I'd not overthrow
That needed me at home to care for them
Because they could not follow where I might go
Or keep me with another stratagem
Than charity. And I have loved you, too,
For being poor in other love and near.
But now I'm blind and satiate with this view,
Far-sighted grown from my fast belvedere.
Ride off, my eyes can't find you for my heart
Until you're fittingly remote, apart.

Pestilence

There is either something wrong with Muldul
Because of the world
Or there is something wrong with the world
Because of Muldul.
They were not born at the same time.
They have no first second to split between them
To keep their time-tongues wagging.
Envy never sold a pack of hounds to age
To lap and yelp at their heels
And be petted with comparisons.
Neither came first.
Neither came afterward.
Both are here,
Present and impetuous.
Time is a timid reservation of immediacy.

The matter is attitude.
One denies Two.
The world lies like gravel in the belly of Muldul

Or Muldul crawls among the bowels of the world,
A conscientious bacillus.
One is sick with the other.

Each is his own physician.
Death will not demonstrate the body.
Death is a dose
But no diagnosis.

Which is inside of which
Is a problem not of life
But of location.
Not Muldul not the world
Has thought more about life
Than a fish bubbling a definition of water.
Life is an element inferred through its creatures.
But place resolves relativity.
Relativity resolves place,
The two around and after each other,
Never, never catching up.

It looks as if Muldul and the world
Can come to no settlement.
Muldul cries with a fever in his side.

The world squirms and scratches its sores
And each ails with the other.

If Muldul spewed up the world,
The world would only say:
At last I have rid me of Muldul.
If the world tore a tumor out of its bowels,
Muldul would boast of good health.

Meanwhile there must be something suffering from both of them
That may be agonizing something else
That agonizes it.

Matter is a complicated complaint of Nothing.
Negation is affirmed in its disorders.
Long life to it!

But what shall be said to Muldul
And what shall be said to the world?

Tell them corruption is its own cure
And they may be grateful for their infirmities.

Pipers

The perennial rats plague the heights.
The words and words will gnaw the red hearts white.
Singers, the hillside down,
Across the moors of misery
Into the sea of poetry
Let the ravening rats speed after you.

Singers and saviors,
Turning dumb away from the shore,
Your silence sucks the red hearts more
White than any rat's tongue,
Bribes a palpitating heart from each
And troops with them over the turf out of reach,
Promising them the sea,
The quick terrible brine of joy bottomless.

Presences

Not as the mechanism of time
Have I held dear the light and dark
But in their manifested prime
Of night and day I can remark

Their presences and sometimes find
The human heart of each beneath
The callous cloak, glimpsing behind
A veil, upon each head, the wreath

Of personality I miss
In other things. I am afraid
There must be some such haze as this
About myself, so overlaid

With being, I must ever pray
That those who pass me by and see
This dim device of living may
Perceive the human heart of me.

Rest

Even the lives my flesh has overlooked,
Even a sin I have not yet done
But am paying for:
Love is the single dying for,
Silently eases the blistered tongue
That hung hysterically long.

And it came, it came,
Fell like a star to stumble on
Across my night,
Waking me utterly,
Putting to sleep
All my lives unatoned,
All the tired lives I have ever lived.

Romantic Profession

Begrimed and smudged with earth –
Oh, grub me up from death,
Forget I had a birth
Who have a prayerful breath.

And I address this plea
Not to a doubtful God
But to a certain me
Crying out of a clod
For immortality.

Myself over the cliff
Will hurl me down to die.
If I'm found stark and stiff
The slayer will be I.

For I won't let me wait,
But dream me here a heaven,
Lest death may be too late
By sixty years or seven
And God the self I hate.

Shores

The river around the secret city of age
Trails like the lank tail of a lazy cat
And that shy smoke of pity hangs about
Whatever fires of diffidence they have
To keep them warm and blinking with the hopes
They have no courage to forsake. Oh dance,
Enduring bones, the flapping, flabby flesh
Is loose and life is lovely for the old,
Hard in their bones forever though death come
A rodent for the meager meat none other
Will touch and trick his scurvy palate with.

Oh dance, if ever you were young as those
Who lower on the farther bank beneath
The swords time swings above each happy head –
These are the scowling young you used to be.
File out on your own bank gaily to-day

In wrinkled, grim grotesque, old dames and fellows,
And cry them to come crossing quickly over,
For death has no more passion here than one
More rattling turn in the last posture of
A tired gavotte. This is the other side
Of humor where philosophy grins small
And wary of too many faiths and trims
Each evangelic wing that had made heaven
Of every disappointment.... Mercy for
Who bide and sing upon the other bank,
Naming the owlish old a watery stretch
Away the enemies of a devout
Eternity youth might encompass in
A singing moment, flying a kite of dreams,
If old age did not dance and drivel and prove
Death is as good as any other way.

Oh dance, oh sing, die young, die old. And peace
On all the shores this river flows between.
There is no moment either on land or sea
Death cannot make into eternity.

Slaves

The universe may be
The whim of a single sultan of eternity.
But the chance chain
Clatters and corrodes
None but a man's rebellious brain.

Beauty forgets the iron ring.
Preoccupation is a free task
And self-acceptance no servitude for skies.
But a man stirs like a cross child,
Listens to the chains of everything,
Tears at his bound brain,
Thinks.

No stricken suns will ever need a bright Jesus.
The order of the winds obeys but beauty.
Truth is the discovery of the allotted duty
And the sufficient custody
Of all but man.

Man wakes. (When was there ever sleep?)
A false dawn breaks.
Pride is the poison of the day.
Untainted the many nights of labor lurk
When after scorn's infliction man must dream and work.

He flees to the prison of his own liberties,
Finds refuge in an unexampled ritual
And chants his deliverance and death
With one breath.

Escape. Farewell you sensible rivers, stars, even beasts.
Courage is unreasoning,
Thought the glorious cowardice.
We might laugh and be brave together
Under a common yoke,
But fear must weep apart, is the new freedom,
The consecrated tyranny
Not of a single sultan
But a whole human agony.

Oh, I'd rather trust a man to the whim of a master
That drives him faster,
Gives him a gold collar, a fair dress,
Than to the slow, kind tortures of himself
That free and strip him ugly to his nakedness.

Sobriety

A goblet is my joy,
Immaculately blown
To sapphire slenderness.

103

Think not that here alone
My solitary cup
I fill with an old wine

And quickly drink it up.
For I shall never taste
My prodigally poured

Sweet draught, but rather haste
To brim its lavish edge
Nor care what surfeit flows

If I but keep my pledge
And never know what lies
Bitterly at the bottom.

Song for a Hot Day

Convey the season to a special climate.
Dispatch the chillest birds we know
To sing the evening
And chirp the morning up.
Bury the sun in silver and then leave it
And in the new nights there will blow
A contradictory spring
Set in the wrong wind's stirrup.

How far can such springs go?
Only as far as summer.
The cool smoke calls the fire.
The trees remember
Where the fruits must grow.
The lull is over and
Your sleep
That could not keep
Forever from its burning land.

Strange....

Pride and the humble heart have been my banners
On different days of this adventuring.
And I have never needed any others
To wave above my wayward soldiering,

But for one enemy that contrived a humor
To give or take not one concerned rebuff.
Strange.... how I stared and stuttered for an answer...
A smile was all I had. Was this enough?

Tears Are a Celebration...

Tears are a celebration
Joy and sorrow must dispute between them.
From the misty smiles of the half-hills,
Down dewy rivers full to their banks,
Come, crafts invisible!
The winds of desire suck up your duel,
Spray you wet to the wept sea
To drift forever over an unthought-of weed
Where unforgivable clings
A lost word that had sunk
Joy and sorrow irreconcilable
In a single peace.

The Magicians

Upon his dais like a rider of
Some dreamy dragon, still, mysterious
And dim, his inward quiet hid from us,
Almost, yet glimmering beneath a veil
Of motion, severe and shaded, Damaryl
Encountered reason and defied it with
Its limitation of achievement and

Its trivial test of possibility,
Declaring it to be a cowardly
Denial of the will. And who could prove
It was not some abracadabra of
Our Damaryl that made a star go out
Or hypnotized the twinning pendulum
Of night and day? If ever fact belied
His prophecies, we said reality
Might make mistakes and trust the cabala
Of time to verify them with a slow
Illusion of remembering. Then why,
We asked, should wonder be made plausible
If time is incident to truth and time
Is esoteric? While the heavens slid,
Astir and shifting with the distant rhythm
Of Damaryl's incantatory song
Over the turning crystal of the moon,
Life was a sleight of sorcery and death
The prestidigitation of reverse
And beauty but a spell of which he held
The talisman – no whittled amulet
Or yet a boar's husk half-bewitched with blood,
But some sweet fetich in the heart enshrined –
Ah, Damaryl, if you had never gone
One day into the mountain's side to try
A harder, more remote enchantment and
Attempt to exorcise the seeming world
Of seemingness and blind the Evil Eye
Of actual sight, until to be became
To be not and to be not was to be,
If you had never bidden us to leave
You practicing a year within that cave,
Imprisoned and imprisoning, we might
Not be to-day the presences of ghosts
You once took from the world and hypnotized.

A year, a year we watched the world to see
Some little sign of difference or yet
The magic trend of transformation, so
Afraid to know whose creatures we might be, –
Existent apparitions of the world
Or proofs of Damaryl or pawns of both –

We could arrive at no high certainty
Of permanence or change or of ourselves.

A year, a year, but Damaryl came not
Again, nor could we find him there beneath
The mountain's crust, a ferret of the cave,
But to the valley ran, whence we had come,
While somewhere an old Evil Eye turned in
Its socket once triumphantly, glinting
The grim charm of a rival conjuror.

The same, the same, by some dazed instinct of
Slow recognition, prizes of the defeat
Of Damaryl and testimonials
Of nothing but ourselves, can it be guessed,
Should some weird accident one day befall
That Evil Eye, what separate wizard sits
In each of us, serene and still and dreaming?

The Mysterious Whoever

A film lies over – not the eyes but over –
The conglomerate, the clouded all
We are in and out of,
Blind both ways.

A crammed socket but an empty eye
Is not too idle, cruel.
Even the imperfect object of a perfect vision
Is faintly food,
For see!

I know of us,
Am not too lonely,
We know of me,
Albeit dimly.

The hunger to behold
Craves more heartily
After a slight startle
When the film falls anew
Upon the ever sudden stranger,
The mediator manifest
Of me to us,
Of us to me,
The mysterious whoever:
You.

The Passionate Women

The passionate women are runners of the hills –
Swift and eager, brief pageant of valleys,
Briefer repose on hilltops,
Taut for to-morrow.
They do not stop long on hilltops:
The passionate women die on hilltops.

But running!
Throats against the wind,
Heads against the sky –
Tremulous throats, high heads –
Lifting the air upon their arms,
Leaning upon their tears,
Leaning upon their hearts,
Hearts untired,
Tired only on hilltops.

These are women:
Only the passionate runners
And the still watchers in the valley.
Both die –
Resting on hilltops,
Running in valleys.

The Pedestal

So still the life of mind has seemed to me,
So still and footed firm upon this rock
That is a pedestal more curiously
Unmoving than myself, I said, "What shock
Of spray, what watery fear, what shove of wave
Can stir me from this place?" How I have cried
A love of quiet and refused a grave
I might have quickly reached but for my pride
In being where I was, not seeing how high
The shifting sea of everything but me
Had risen about my rock, not until I
Was covered, not until the enemy
I had defied flooded the height and claimed
My pedestal and me! But O! so still
And footed firm . . . . For this shall we be named
Forever, we fettered two. No water's will
Or shove of wave can carry one along, –
Myself, or yet this rock that is my song.

The Rapture

To cry the grief away
Would cry away the rapture
I could never recapture
When I had wept me gay.

I laugh. Intactly burns
The sorrow, not a flicker
Bends the flame or makes quicker
The time a memory turns

Not backward, but ahead,
Where my rapture waits me dead.

The Saint of Daros

He tapped the rocks until they all ran dry
And licked unsavoring the local sky
Clean of what clouds could pity his real thirst
And with real rain undo a parched vow curst
With an unreal denial. Swiftly out
Of sky and rock and marsh, saddened with doubt,
Love leaked away to disbelief and hate
That drained to drought the heart of Hilgan's sin
And left a withered pulse on the fain din
Of haunted chastity drumming the mumble
Of a fanatic faith too harshly humble
With an unkind austerity to give
A blessing by which he might better live.

Alandrome was love, but love was stuff
Of her, and he had sworn to be enough
Himself for him. She was too large with space
That distanced him and brought the sweet disgrace
Of gratitude for what he had not been
Without herself to spread his substance in.
For no old quarrel forgotten in their flesh
And found in love and reinstated fresh
In their renewed hostility, did he
Fly out the nest where fleet Alandrome
Had taught him flying; but beginning then
A hate new in her death and old again
If Hilgan died to meet her anywhere
Outside of Daros, unremarked and fair
Not separately, ringed with a radiance
Of death she could not darken or enhance
To dim his halo to dependence or
Bless him with light he must be grateful for.

Fed to the panting rocks of Daros, she
Splashes a rain and floods a river he
Will never hear, remembering how his soul
Recoiled from her and broke the brimming whole
Her swimming surfeit made of him and thrust
His body on her to murder her with lust.

110

Now Hilgan drinks no drop of anything
In Daros and his hoarse throat cannot sing
The thick tongue's thirst. Oh, holy loveless man
Who found a quiet craving saintlier than
Stifling fulfillment: saved by sacrifice
From sin that had been able to suffice,
Canonized by himself for a cruel fate
Of crippled love that love had twisted straight.

The Same Small Way

The careless clues to other passions than ours
Lie all about.
But there's no knowing or devining of them
Save we must doubt,
Seeing that they are large and can mean little,
Our own intent
In an old spirit that must sign for all
One sacrament.

Even the four winds, since they blow, have souls
And are amazed
How they are caught among the fiends and furies
That must have blazed
Their unspent immortality before,
Lighting the fires
Of every quiet and martyrizing men
On their desires.

Whether the sorrow is universal, then,
Or if we share
Love with lilies or the earth itself –
I cannot bear
The anguish any better, I am swept
The same small way
Toward disappearance and a more immense
Fever of decay.

The Shore

No water-dragon of the sea I sail
Can prove his fatal fins on me.
Creamy the useless morning scares the gale
Of dark I feared indifferently.

For I have not a finger-joint or rib
To crack and split the wind that shrieks
Exasperated in and out the jib,
Nor eyes to clear the sky it streaks.

Some time too soon this thin and painless wave
That thought never a shore to see
Will founder frightfully upon the grave
Of flesh that bears my agony.

The Spider

Just right, more, or less, –
Skinny Spider,
Leave me unspun out of this.

You and I secretly
Need only know the true size of the cloth
Reduced by me.

Spider, don't spin away
Your whole body,
Let me stay

Here unwound and unwoven
To bury after
Six old legs crooked, cloven,

Watch the angelic butterfly
Crawling on the finished carpet
Where never I

Shall squirm
Threaded in unalterable homage
Beneath each everlasting worm.

Spider, Spider, let me be,
Because unventured,
The heaven of
Arachne,
Her humility
And private penance,
Wise and actual end
Of a long legendary folly.

The Stone

The simple and the gentle knew this shrine
And came to kiss the amethystine stone
That beat the heart of it miraculously,
Purple and cold it lay upon its cloth.
Yet what importance glinted certainly
Within the secret shadowy gloom of it!
A woman wept and went away consoled.
It sparkled on a corpse and lighted death
To a lugubrious life, and chilled the fires
And fevers of the hundred livid hates
And of the one pale love. And it was kind
And had no preferences for a prince
Against a pauper but the pity of
A stone for what was soft and flaccid flesh.
It never shone astonished on a hurt
A man might think too queer and cruel to heal.
It seemed no spirit mystical of man,
But only the dry principle of change.
The melancholy pilgrims sped home gay.
Each roisterer gained sadness and a soul.
And many a peace it made, but was not peace
Itself; unspun the long entanglement,
The miserable mesh of twisted fact;
Set the slave free, adrift upon himself;

113

Lifted the veil of sleep that dreams might be
Truly beheld in sight.... What was this stone?
A thing dug out of the earth and set in a shrine,
Its magic not the power that it gave
To men, but all the human power that
Men greatly granted it, only the sign
Of man's high cowardice, afraid to face
Himself unmirrored in a god or stone
And see the might that lies in him alone.

The Subterfuge

They called Philander Solomon and not
In any waggish way of derogating
His dignity, but that he had likewise
Been questioned by the Lord and had but sought
An understanding heart, eschewing riches
In that he loved them not and honor, too,
Preferring that poor fame that men might give,
Knowing it would then be more stubbornly
Deserved since God was kindlier than men.
They called him Solomon and only once
Had called him king, for he had said, "I may
Be Solomon, good friends, but I have read
Tom Paine and can't be king and I have watched
The trees and learned there is no preference
In leaves, but that one falls as freely as
The other. And I would not be mayor or
The lowliest yet of those who are only
A little less lowly than the lowliest.
For there is that in power that will lure
The bravest democrats to cowardly
Dominion of usurped authority,
And I would rather sit upon my steps
A hundred years and modestly smoke there
My thoughtful, unaspiring pipe than be
A mighty monarch for a royal day
That might encompass in a sovereign way
What is illiberally done in one

114

Ignoble lifetime." And then those who heard
Him hung their smile indulgently on a
Respectful seriousness because they knew
Philander had more empire over them
Than if he wielded some badged sinecure.
For mayors were as days – when one went down
There was another one impatiently
Upon his heels. And kings were harnessed to
Their ministers and so must run apace
With them and not a step beyond lest there
Be found a beast more tractable. But old
Philander only talked and sculptured thoughts
With words until they gently shaped themselves
To mastery and listeners became
Lieutenants then for their accomplishment.
And so when their Philander sat for one
Ungoverned week and did not speak a word
For their administration, they were sure
That when Philander spoke at last there would
Be words enough to make all those dumb days
Magnificently eloquent. There were.
Philander laid his pipe upon the step
As if enough reflection had been voiced
In silent smoke. "Good neighbors, are we not
All democrats and would we then allow
One man among us to abide in office
A little longer than his portioned time
Were he as sternly just as God himself?
And presidents have their appointed hour
And kings and all kings' sons have theirs beyond
Renomination. So I ask and yet
Ask reverently: Who elected God?
Or, if we call Him King, I wonder that
There is none other of His dynasty
To be a young successor to old realms.
But if you say He is immortal, I
Will know that you prefer eternities
Of tyranny to short successive terms
Of democratic deity and love
The timid comforts of old habits then
Far better than a new republic of
The universe and canvass favors of

115

Your God to pay for a lost liberty."
In their town now, the last of May, because
It seems to be a month for candidates
And buds ambitious for their offices,
When all the jolly citizens of spring
Go casting votes for summer, they declare
A celestial election day to see
Who will be Lord the coming year and they
Are very careful now whom they inscribe
Upon that other ticket against God
Since that first time they asked Philander to
Accept the nomination and he said
With a wry gravity, "I'm sorry, neighbors,
I can't compete with God to be the Lord,
For I might be elected then and if
I were I'd speedily resign in favor
Of Him that knows His business better than
Myself or any other, and that would be
A matter of some embarrassment to Him
And me. And don't you either now resort
To nominating babbling simpletons
To make the vote unanimous, as if
You thought that God was a lodge president."
Since then they've always nominated some
Good clergyman to be a running mate
To God, knowing he'll have the votes of all
His congregation, yet assured that all
The rest of us will have the sense to see
Which of the two would make the fitter Lord,
Enough at any rate to give to God
A reverent majority. Thus did
They prove their principles and keep their God.

The Sweet Ascetic

Find me the thing to make me less
Delivered to my earthliness,
Some rarer love to live upon,
A berry grown in Avalon,
Something that will, in this emprise,
Suffice me to etherealize
The coarser strain and purify
The flesh that had preferred to die.

Find me this thing and plant it near
My garden gate so that some day,
When I am going out of it,
I'll stoop to pick the ripest bit
And, humming as I walk away,
Smile just a little and disappear.

The Twins

The original mother
Bore nothing but twins.

Misery came only a moment earlier
Than merriment from the womb.

It is this moment
That makes us possible.

Should we be less impartial than their mother,
Keep one company, ostracize the other?

Their souls are similar.
She did but dress them differently
To tell them apart.

These Men Have Been....

These men have been
Bold men and great:
That Macedonian,
Caesar,
Napolean.
They have taken for steeds
Their heroical deeds
And say they'll ride farther in fame
Than in time.

Most men have not been
Bold men and great.
Most men are content
With caution to wait
And with their last breath
Mount an old mare called death
That rides safely ahead
Into time with her dead

And won't keep coming back
With a maggoty pack
Like the steeds
That were deeds
Of that Macedonian,
Caesar,
Napolean.

Timothy's Lad

He must teach the child.

(They said he was the man.
Hadn't he been to Hindustan?
Won three decorations in the war?
– Did they know what for –)

But nothing too true, too wild.

Does David know where dead men go?
The opposite way when they're alive.
Which way was that?

Timothy mustn't frighten him so.

Couldn't you teach anything to a child?

Only the little things like stars.
The dangerous peace in David's eyes
Had a demon behind.
It's this we're afraid of, Timothy.

Timothy tried.

But David grew up and never died
Cleanly as everyone else,
But wore out like a book,
Never lost that look....

It was Timothy's fault.

(But what did they want of a child that was born
While his father was off at war?)

To a Proud Lover

Until you have beheld her truly,
All she is,
The white wonder,
Out to the last prospect of her mysterious mind,
You cannot have her.

Her loving can but be
Your love's best vision of her
When the black bulbs
Will be unlidded, sprout sight.

Love is no invasion.
Do but comprehend, where you stand,
That her head is amplified in air,
That her hands include what they touch,
Lose not what they drop.
Under her the earth's appulse
Knots her with an infinite,
With what is next.

There is no need to laugh when she laughs,
There is no need to look where her eyes leap,
To accompany her.
There is no way to win her with art.
Care would be clumsy, even sinful.
Do but see simply the white wonder she is,
The many bright musics,
The appearance symphonic.

Yet how can you ever
Traverse your swart soul?
Bloom her freely enough
From your unfraught bulbs
That beblack and screen her candor,
Bebarren the all-implicit vision?

To see her purely
Who can see but darkly,
You must see her not at all,
You must have her not at all.

Unpour your pride.
Bid the very vessel thin,
Shred to receive her
As light not liquid,
As the pervading grace
Of your destruction
In the possession.

To This Death

I shall be lover to the earth.
It will delight her to know her body this way.

I shall amaze her with discoveries of herself,
Stirring the little pools that were too clear,
Clipping what grew too swiftly close to her heart again.

Nevermore impure and unagonized,
Nevermore loveless and teeming,
Barren and tumid mother of the barren.

I shall use love like a knife upon her,
Whittling her down till one stroke would lose her,
Spare for suffering,
Able to bear my single seed only.

Oh, flower of pain!
To this fruition have I brought the earth,
To this death.

Transmigration

You are tall and straight, Eileen,
Haughty in your bib and cap, –
Something like a Celtic queen,
Pods for jewels in your lap.

When you bear a hot tureen,
I forget and would arise.
You are like a secret queen
With those cold contemptuous eyes.

Was I not a poor colleen
Long ago, a live-long while,
Handmaid to a gray-eyed queen,
Mistress of a mighty Isle?

Tratch

Wrapped Tratch crackling in brown paper,
Buried him crisply into the tricky trap
That snapped death's device efficiently
Before flies smacking their lacks
Slippery along mysterious manila
Could buzz the nozzling ecstacy
Of taste intoxicated accurately.
For Tratch died of good health in a sick world,
Rolled plump over the precipice of strength,
Collapsed crushed on a feather-bed.

Flumed down the dizzy chute,
Tuned to the slow snapping
Of the arch of an owl's whistle
That had hooted the prophecy of all this
The night he died, and rustling in his wrapper
The lorn accompanying undertone
Imitating the lament of two lovers below
Disturbed immortally in death
By an immortal celebration of song above:

"Life bedded them
And they arose
To dawn and death."

Tratch dropped on them cursing the prying poet,
Excused himself, said: "I quite agree with you,"
Unparceled him, papered the lovers in his sheet
And shot them up the chute nobody knows
Whatever happened to them.

Tratch turned, trimmed his tongue for a speech
To quiet the emaciated clamoring fellow dead
Starved by the stinted lives they'd led
With no provisioning for death.

"Here I am, speckless, undisordered.
Life was very honest when the time came,
Gave as much of me back as it originally absorbed,
Charged me nothing for the fruity women

I only nibbled negligently and left to rot.
I say things are statistically
Better than in your day. Fewer
Quarrels with the dead, and working women
Hoard secret certainties of queenship.
Love is a little more unprecedented,
New kinds of kissing; and right-hand kitchen-cooking
Improvises left-hand dreams.
Piece by piece courage is being purged of lies,
Left with the last truth of the twin chaos
Life and death bearing each other eternally.
Oh, we are aware up there seriously
Of the spatial nonsense of separation.
Once electrically myself loving a bright lady
I bridged a conventional chasm
And destroyed traditional distance.
Only a part I played, of course.
Death is the off-stage in the wings.
Ladies and gentlemen,
I crave a little professional applause."

But they put Tratch aside impatiently,
Tearing with the greeting courtesy of greed
The twine and tissue of a new package just arrived,
Unwrapped another Tratch,
Shrieked successive disappointment
Over a Tratch epidemic,
Grumbled sullen submission when someone said
Tratch was a Prophet with a following,   .
Never noticed the grinning hum-hum and no more
Every Tratch spoke to every Tratch
Or hissed the inaugural speech
Every Tratch made to all of them.

Newspapers the next morning stammered
Seventy-seven suicides of men
Scientifically cured of death.

Nobody anywhere understood.
Something should have been said about habit.

Trinity

Seeds are the flesh of flowers
And every sun a soul.
Rain splashed a death of hours.
Together a triple whole
Might blossom fresh
Immortal mesh
Of mortal three
Eternally.

I
Sowing

Wherefrom with earth away
Blew starry winds these singing seeds
Into the reckless flash
Fast in the sprouting fields of time
But with no suns or rains but one another?

No old confession can smother
An older heritage of doubt
Rooted in alien dust
And peaked in petals upward thrust
Only in sad disdain upon belief.

Whatever heights of grief
They blossom to bloom but to bend
Hungering close upon
The trafficked radiance and rain
A common mercy doles their separate pain.

II
The Garden of Drought

Around the garden slept a sea
    Unfollowable far.
Dreams of a wind and a wave
Wounded the still with no scar
That held its lone divinity
    Of death like a wet star
Heavened in the sunken grot of its grave.

But in the garden crackled the seeds,
 Shone white through the black earth,
Filled to a flower each petal,
Fashioned a ray of each nettle,
And woke their souls to suns, dried weeds
 Of doubt and budded reeds
Bright from the barren grass of their birth.

"But where is rain?" the flowers cried,
 Implored each seed and sun
Wedded to blossom in one.
Marriage is mortal, unfree
Of thirst. But ever is trinity.
 And they unborn of three
Blew toward the blessed water and died.

III

Rain

The seeds lifted their suns and made a sky
And flowers parched between.
Gray was the green,
Rivery ran the earth
But overflowing dry
In oceanic dearth.

The flowers stole a prayer from their desire
And wilted into faith
Doubt made a wraith.
Clouds crumbled then each sun
And rain fell from their fire
Like a last benison.

No second prayer could bring suns back again.
Faith floated where it drank,
Faith fed and sank.
Forfeited was the light
To turn a desert of pain
Into a sea of night.

IV
Sun and Sea

All petaled personalities
Clocked the raindrops into timeless seas,
Resolved their suns swimmingly
Into a current goldenly
Edging a borderless main
That flooded the full leas
And made a landless plain

Of land, drowned deep and dank the seeds,
Freed the flowers into water-weeds
Rootless on waves lazily
With spray and sun-foam hoping to
Have heaven echoing through
The tides lost, shoreless, free
A woundless ocean bleeds.

But death lies in the water and
Weds with neither sun nor seeded sand
And flowers live lifelessly
Upon the surface seedlessly,
Bring new blossoms to birth
Unbodied of the land,
Souled, deathed, but dead of earth.

V
Event

Now, seeds religiously
Pray through to air,
Break their buds full and free
To flower and prayer.

Now individually
The love-bees swarm
And suns are sweet and holy,
Scent flowers warm.

126

And wet and musically
The sea striates
The land unfloodingly
Nor inundates,
Though death, soul, body, sun and seed,
But is the word
Of the halved, doubled creed,
And singing third.

VI
Celebration

Love rose a wind and like a wind
        And was the thing
That married body and soul and death
        And was the breath
Of blessing on the wedding.

Love ribboned in and out to bind
        And blew between
Each sun and seed and raining sea
        Thrice timelessly
Turned earth aquatic, sea terrene,

And dipped the sun brightly in both
        Till now flowers grow
Not parented so separately
        And mortally,
But waving ever in love's blow.

Oh I am loath
To say the seed the body and God and life
And death the ebbing agony of Christ's strife,
Call every sun and soul the Host
        Lighting the Holy Ghost.

Let love alone be named
Unnamable wind and what,
Baptismal secret of the babes begot
In flowery mystery
        Unshamed
Out of an unidentifiable trinity.

127

Triumph

Sight is the flashing trick of blindness.
The clogged eyes estop
The gushing vision of ultimate flux.

The flooded ears spill eternal sonatas,
Deaf and splashing gutter-gurgling.

Limp, limp, lame with legs,
Faith stumbling-still still hour on hour
Over faith instant with wings.

The spite of self in the dumb tongue
Stuffs the tuned throat with the wool of words,
Gags the angry message in the mouth.

Life alive and stilted.
Breath the suffocation of the spirit.
Existence deadlock.

Death the divine contradiction of self-defeat.

Grotesque triumph!

Truth's Promise

To-day is.
To-morrow must be.
The burden of necessity
Is never now.

Truth's promise
Bears beyond all actual.
Go we must
Toward the test,
Establishing more days
For more morrows.

Two Hells

I
Of Prometheus

No suns or seas weather this world
Heavenless where the skies are furled.
The fixed eyes stare never at a star,
There is no possible of far
But the impossible parade
Of close crimes only man has made.
The fate of an ungrateful guest
Follows you, fiend, from the spurned rest
Earth gave, into the catacomb
Of pride that is your lasting home.

II
Of Damon

Overly friend, Damon, and fool, –
Hell is the fire and horrible school
Where life is taught too late the trust
Of life, that can be broken for lust
Or love, betrayed, yet sin forgiven.
But to have served, Damon, and striven
Neither for woman nor love, but man,
This is a false faith that you can
Expiate only madly now
Over and over with each new vow
And each new friend of fire that will
In his red kiss your pledge fulfill.

Underground

The roots we are
Turn up,
Turn down,
Alive, alive and underground.

Downward magnetized,
Fastened with mysteries,
The dark springs under
And weather over
Maybe to flower in.

But in between
A fatted soil to fatten in.

The gormandizing appetite
Nibbles too long along the way
And sickens the seed's old lust of light.

Now asleep and slow –
We'd rather grow than go –

And guzzled and tuberous and sodden
The delicate veins that might have tunneled
In tendril trains to flowers
We might have been.

Turn over.
Sleep.
Alive and underground is well.
But underground and dead,
Well-fed
In Eden and Hell –

For shame,
Vegetables!

Waste

Cruel then too exquisite to be cruel,
The bright wheel of the body's breaking
Whirls and attunes
The self-ecstatic flesh
To other torture.
It is not death.
Death is too sober.
Death permits no martyr.

The destined rack
That never may be actual,
The full infliction unattainable
In pain but partial:
It is a dream
Of hope rather than horror.
And how shall we rejoice in death
That wastes the one abiding power?

Xenones and Kyranos

These were two men
Blithely abhorrent to each other.
Their hates were sober cloaks
Draped gravely over them,
Else this long while
There would have been but one of them.

They did not hate for women or for gold
Or for a word unwisely aimed to wound.
No man could say what made them hate,
But only that one fatal morning
They walked into the town,
One luminously from the east,
One darkly from the west,
To meet upon the market-place
And look profoundly in each other's eyes,
And looking, hate.
And they were more endeared in hate
Than they had ever been in fellowship –
Two courteous hates,
Two deferential hates
That bowed urbanely to each other
And dearly kept their brotherhood,
For saving hate, these men had little else
To recommend them to each other,
Xenones being fat and loose of tongue,
Kyranos meanly framed and grimly worded.

And so they met and talked
And chided yet if one had been
Unfaithful to their enmity
In some fond, foolish word with others,
Until one day came oily-spoken, great-paunched Chalon
To upbraid them in a priest's unknowing way
Of running all the errands of the Gods
To their old dun-faced maiden aunts the fates,
And stroke his hands as if to wring
Some fair divinity from them:
"Oh, come, my friends," – and that was wisely spoken,
For they were friends indeed,
Such as no knuckle-knotted hands of an old seer
Could make them with a miserly annointment
Of scant grace – "I come but now
From Delphi where I went
To hear what plan of peace
The oracle might there propound
For your tranquility and for our own –
For omens have been sent me,
Portentous dreams in which
Pylades struggled with Orestes
And Damon strove with Pythias
And two fair mottled heifers
Gamboled in our streets together.
It seemed that I came out and stroked their noses
Until the face of one
Took on the image of the other,
While through the streets an eerie bruit
Went chuckling that old Chalon
Had devised a miracle –
A mocking dream that leered behind my eyes
Until the young moon found a stout old age
And all the melancholy stars
Came weeping to her funeral
And then it was I went to Delphi's priestess
To hear what gossip the mighty-winded gods
Had lately whispered in her ears.
'What word, oh gracious lips of heaven?'
I cried, 'What presage for
Xenones and Kyranos?'
But from the chasm beneath her rose a laugh,

A wild, familiar laugh so like
That one that once had coiled
Insidiously through the streets to plant
Its fangs in my bewilderment, that I
Could little tell which one of those
Had been the echo of the other.
But she was grave, as grave
As old men are before young wit.
'Go back, good Chalon,
Let them change their names
For one moon's brief endurance of the sky,
And breathing thus each other's breath,
And quickening to each other's pulse,
They'll rift the fragile mantles of their souls
And come to such dim understanding as
The fates allow this side of Stygian reaches.'
This was her bidding that I give you now
Unscathed by any advocacy of
My own, save what unwitting warmth
Of piety may make my words
More faithful to her ordinance
Than to my own unprepossessed intention."

Xenones and Kyranos smiled
And in their smile found gay agreement
With Chalon's bashful exhortation
And stood with pleasant seriousness
While Chalon gently stroked them with
A hopeful incantation
As many dreams ago he stroked
The faces of two darling heifers
To a delighted difference.
And there was no one witness to both sights
To say that Chalon's words
Were more persuasive than his fingers.
But there were two beloved foes
Who knew that each had magically come
To be the other one of them.
"And go you now," old Chalon bade them,
"And if the gods be willing,
Affectionately learn to read
The tangled traceries of each other's ways,

And having read, roll up your separate scrolls,
Return to your old selves again
Grown fondly wise in an old lore of hate."

That one enlivened moon
Delayed then its reluctant wane,
For this play was the drollest that
She ever had beheld.
At last Xenones, he that once had been
Kyranos, and Kyranos, that had been
Xenones once, kept their appointed tryst
With Chalon, who straightway turned
His ample back on them to be
A wall between themselves and heaven
While he harangued the gods to change
These two into their former selves,
To see what miracle of love
Their whilom habitation of
Each other's self had wrought.

And Chalon spoke and turned and turning cried
And crying madly importuned the gods
To make them what they had once been
Before they were transformed
Into what they were not.

But with amused solemnity
They obdurately stood
And would not be redeemed again.
For in that pleasant moon
Xenones grew to love
Kyranos' thin severity so much
And lean Kyranos came to be
So radiantly enamoured of
Xenones' sweet complacency
That they refused to be
Delivered to themselves again,
But left old Chalon grieving there
While they walked sportively away,
Happy in a new flesh and an old hate.

And Chalon stood agape and grieved
For their perverse, irreverent whim,
And as he grieved it seemed a wily laugh
Came mocking his bereaved anticipations.
He wondered then what laugh it was,
That one that had pursued him in a dream,
Or that that had arisen like
A smoke from the Delphic abyss
So perilously mounted by an oracle,
Or yet the wrinkled laugh
Of three old maiden aunts
Spinning with tidy accuracy.

III

A Kindness

To be alive is to be curious.
When I have lost my interest in things
And am no more alert, alacritous
For fact, I'll end this bated enquiry.
Death's the condition of supreme ennui.

I shall permit me to disintegrate
And then, because I know the peace death brings,
It will be good to keep persuading fate
To be more generous, extending, too,
This privilege of boredom to all of you.

Abstainer

Only enough scum
For my mouth to scale a minimum
Of the spare soul's diet
And keep the clamoring epicure quiet.

I don't want much.
The less life's asked to give
The less I'm pledged to live.
Chary upon my sulking crutch,
I'll hobble and click and grudge the reluctant me
That pays a piddling toll for what it is afraid entirely not to be

Adorned

Too high here on this quiet crag
To find the world food
If it fruited toward me and fell
Mellowly into my mouth
And fawned on my tongue;
Yet, since I am a man and king and young,

Drift, world, over my rood
And I will make you the first gem
Shining out of my diadem
And crown of death.

Adventure in a Train

Iron jaws, devourers of space,
Machine of my hope!
Might I kiss you,
If you had some secret heart to hide me in,
A little cold hollow where I could keep me warm
And tunnel and runnel you with my own blood
Till you were mad and I the soul of madness.....

Ah, love!
Together the blind beast, we,
Dead flesh and my living spirit,
Together the dragon of distance, we –
Ah, love!
To the end, to the end,
Through city, through field, –
Stop for no wildflower tangled in your jaws,
For no mixed masonry of bone and stone.
I am the furnace,
I am the soul,
I cannot be forgotten for these.

To the end, love, we are come,
To the rim of reasonable things.
Gravity is the parting protest of the widowed earth.
Farewell!
Off!

Stop for no star.
Run over the sun.
Grind up a universe, if you must.

Festooned with comets,
Splashed with this nebular mud,
Free and crazy –
Stop, stop, they cry!
Impossible!
We're looking for a track
To take us back
To the earth again.
We would rather wake up at home.

Against Adventure

I went away one day
As something that was usually me
To have a certain way
Of knowing just how usual things could be,
And ordinarily fair,
Alone, without me there.

And in no place at all,
And for no minute moving on a clock,
I rested and let fall
Upon that unwonted seclusion the lock
Of individual strife
Marking the separate life.

Somehow myself returned.
Nothing had even forgotten my right name,
And not a leaf had learned,
Through missing me, to be never the same
Upon a different tree,
Half-changed through me;

But I alone a thing
Touched with this unaccountable time apart
And back with me bringing
Only a record of age I could not chart
On any travel-table
Of the eternal fable.

Which one of us shall yet
Defeat the human folly of abstraction
Must conquer the regret
For fresh adventure lost to used inaction
Where all may live less bold,
But where none can die old.

An Ancient Revisits

They told me, when I lived, because my art
To them seemed wide and spacious as the air,
That time would be pervaded everywhere
With it, until no work would have a part
That had not once awakened in my heart,
That everything would crooked be or fair
As it inherited its proper share
From me and could that share again impart.
But this strange present world is not of me.
If I could find somewhere a secret sign,
That one might say: In this an Ancient sings,
I should acknowledge then my legacy
And love to call this modern fabric mine.
Perhaps, once, in my sleep, I dreamed such things?

An Easier Doom

Wide as a pavement is the moment,
Too pearly,
Its light of a sun made most for heavens,
Not earthly.

Overpetted, I purr along it,
Too many walk it,
Too many friends and freedoms fill it:
It is too wide, too long.

Were it a single spot,
And so suddenly,
Were it no common highway
But mine utterly
And soil only enough to stand on,
Set in the mark
Of its own dark –

Ah, what is this I ask,
A lonely wilderness of me forever?
Mine is an easier doom
As this poor passing creature
With a few streets to be crossed over,

Blessed with company and light
And an alien pity
Till the last turning,
The unsuspected stepping-off
Into the perpetual space
Where I become terribly
Not myself.

Angelica

Dirty bugger,
Swells around the corner
Never saw her.

Diamond in the rough,
Not a polished bluff,
But the real stuff.

Scuttling city elf,
Kept her tongue on the shelf,
Sang only to herself.

And her mother was a bum
And her father too drank some.
She was scum.

143

And her birth was unrecorded.
All the secrecy she hoarded
That an alley afforded.

Garbage was her rosary,
And flesh the martyry
Where garbage came out flowery.

What should she have been doing
Instead of brewing
Silver out of gutter-spewing?

Let her lurk
In the murk
Doing divine dirty work.

If God left her out of Creation,
Then God atoning in Damnation
Will find her Heaven and Salvation.

Or if he meant to leave her in,
Her blasphemy becomes His sin,
His purgatory all her vermin.

This is Angelica,
Singing through scrofula,
May she survive even Utopia.

Anniversary

We are old, we are old,
We are a voyage old, you and I.

A long tramp we made together,
With you carrying me in your arms when the rain was deep.

There were great trees in the road.
Sometimes I hid from you behind them.

There were great stones in the road.
We sat down on them, kicking feet in the dust.

When we were hungry food somehow came,
And we ate it hilariously, there on the road.

I remember once we were tired
And rested seriously under the stars.

Sometimes you looked into my eyes
And gave me a slow, solemn kiss.

More often we were pelting each other
With flowers we picked on the road.

Wild sunsets, there were, too.
We watched them silently, with tight hands.

Even an old dead beggar we passed on our way.
We buried him and loved on his grave.

Oh, we knew how to be selfish,
Passing folks by with our pockets full.

But we did our share of weeping for others,
There on the long road in the darkness.

For ourselves, it didn't much matter
Whether we were laughing or crying.

It was all on the road, on the road.

Another Apple

Take care what piece of me you take to taste,
And prove me on no individual bite.
How many times your stupid mouth must waste
My fruit until it learns that even despite
My single rind no sample is the same

To eat and test me on, I shall but wait,
Fearing what hungry chance may yet inflame
The tooth's sharp appetite and drive it straight
Through this composite, non-committal meat
Into the secret and astringent core
Where bitter and entire this gall shall greet
The tongue's first touch. And you will need no more
To know me well and ever and thoroughly.
Short wit to who make their last meal of me.

Ars Mortis

Listen for the voices to cry *danger*!
Then you may go.
Where the most rash entrusting
Tempts foreboding,
Fly to the monster,
Lean to its fierce heart low,
Enable it to own you,
Defy the fire in its kiss
With a dear name a cinder and a silence soon.
Such love is not a savagery
But how angels must choose
To reach heaven a shorter way
Spiriting up from hell swiftly
As Satan fell into it.

Most frightening is the hour that holds
And will not care.
The loves that come like moths to it
Will tease around it, taste not of it,
Fall down unfed when feeding were redeeming.
It burns – what is it to be safe and smoke?
It is still until still no longer,
Is gone nowhere and not given over
To its time to elude it.
Only what is staked is saved.
Only what is lost makes elsewhere.
Death can be full of findings

Or black as nothing of brightness kept
In covert, never ventured,
When it was life.

There is too much of us.
Sparing is waste.
Confess the excess
To the serpents just beyond
In the passes upon Helicon,
That will devour the offering,
Then sing up all the braves
In an immortal size proportionate to courage,
The love of death, the worship of a larger life
Where faith is matched with form
And we are all muses.

Bacchus

Pandio wove the laughing leaf in his hair.
Pandio danced up his vineyard slope.
Pandio's big-eyed berries gleamed darkly through the leaves,
Watching how he ran up to meet the hilltop,
Watching how the hilltop crept down to meet him.

The sun came down to meet them, too,
The eagle sun with a lark on its wing.
(Bacchus jumped from the sun's cold back and cried:
"It's time to hide your face in the night,
The withering moon is on the way.")

Bacchus lay in a flat-armed tree,
Tying his ivy-tangled feet on a branch,
And fell asleep
And listened to Pandio's song in a dream.

"Hear! Bacchus,
Silver-eyed Bacchus,
Bacchus of the grape-stained lips.
Your breast is the breast of a virgin
And your feet are knuckled like the hands of an old man.

"Hear! Bacchus.
Your heart is dyed in an old wine.
Your blood is purple as the wings of the sun.
Your body is woman-white,
Like the dew-cup of the morning.

"Bacchus! Bacchus!
The big eyes of my berries
Sleep no more at night.
(In the spring their lids were closed all day.)

"Summer has begun to forget
And the dryads are growing old again.

"There is not much time left, Bacchus,
There is not much time left."

Pandio climbed into a flat-armed tree
And fell asleep
And heard an answer in his dreams.

"Pandio, Pandio.
There is a white goat skipping your hill
With a coat for a wine-skin.
There are light-footed young girls
Dancing upon their desires in the valley.
Let them stamp as wildly upon your grapes,
Pressing a dangerous wine,
Dark and sweet with young wickedness and wishes.

"I will set my lips upon it,
Making it darker yet
To hide an older madness.

"Pandio, Pandio.
I will give you hoofs for hopping
And teach you how to mount the back of the sun
When you are tired.
I will fasten your wine skin round your neck
With a naiad's hair.
I will give you a satyr's vine-twisted staff
That is berry-crowned.

"Pandio, Pandio.
There will be none like, then,
To make the world drunk
And merry and mad and worshipful
For Bacchus' sake,
And glad for the wine of life
And glad for the wine of death.

"Pandio, Pandio.
They say:
      Bacchus is growing old
      Spring comes too late
      Autumn comes too soon.
      Grapes are dusky and dim on their vines.
      Bacchus is growing old,
      Bacchus is dying.
      Aphrodite has no white myrtle blossoms
      For her hair.
      Bacchus has grown too old for gardening,
      Bacchus will soon be dead.

"Pandio, Pandio.
Can winter freeze the sun?
Can summer melt the moon?
Can age and death avail
Against Bacchus –
Bibber of many wines,
Quaffer of many lives,
Gardener of many hillsides?

"Pandio, Pandio.
The earth prays to the gods of sorrow.
The earth prays to the gods of despair.
The old, gay earth is soberly dying.
Go, make the earth drunk.
Go, make the earth fair."

*   *   *

After a busy time
Pandio hung his wine skin on his neck
And walked up into Thessaly with his staff

149

Or hopped on his new-grown hoofs
Or sat astride on the sun when he was tired.

Pandio met an old god in a forest.
"Have you heard," the god said,
"That Bacchus is growing old?
Perhaps he is dead
By this time."

Pandio sighed
And offered the god
A jowlful of wine.

The old god drank
And tasted his lips.
The old god drank and drank again.
"Perhaps Bacchus is younger than I thought.
You should drink some of this wine yourself, little man."

That night two danced tipsily
In a forest in Thessaly
And one had hoofs
And one danced on the air.

That night two slept
Under a tree in Thessaly
With an empty wine skin under their heads
And one was a god
And one was dead.

That old god woke to a mellow youth
And folded the wine skin under his arm
And looked for Bacchus, to fill it up,
On every hillside in Thessaly,
Singing a little song
That he learned one night
From a little man
Who danced too long.

"The earth prays to the gods of sorrow.
The earth prays to the gods of despair.
The old, gay earth is soberly dying.

Go, make the earth drunk.
Go, make the earth fair."

* * *

There are two races of gods now.
There are the gods of sorrow and despair.
They grow older and older in their heaven and never die.
They keep saying:
    Bacchus is growing old
    Spring comes too late.
    Autumn comes too soon.
    Grapes are dusky and dim on their vines.
    Bacchus is growing old,
    Bacchus is dying.
    Aphrodite has not white myrtle blossoms
    For her hair.
    Bacchus has grown too old for gardening,
    Bacchus will soon be dead.

There are the other gods.
(Some say their sire danced long ago.)

They walk on earth,
Holding an empty wine skin up for filling,
Singing a little song
That old sire learned one night
From a little man
Who danced too long.
    "Can winter freeze the sun?
    Can summer melt the moon?
    Can age and death avail
    Against Bacchus,
    Bibber of many wines,
    Quaffer of many lives
    Gardener of many hillsides?

    "The earth prays to the gods of sorrow.
    The earth prays to the gods of despair.
    The old, gay earth is soberly dying.
    Go, make the earth drunk,
    Go, make the earth fair."

151

Somewhere
Bacchus lies asleep in a flat-armed tree,
With his ivy-tangled feet tied on a branch,
Hearing songs across his dreams....

Bed-ease

When no more wonderful is misery a horror,
The awakened neck sings not unhappy against the shoulder,
Sleeps to the pillow of a sob
And does not shriek, now home,
Now home the fright out of the street,
Stripped to the feeble flesh of sorrow.
The body is its own relic and not lyrical,
Lies like an innocent troll
With tears made plain and beautiful.
The human manikin of soul
Speaks strange and nothing in the Square.
But horror is abed
Marveling to be itself in arms and legs and lying
Close with comfort very sad.

Belaguna

In Belaguna, in Belaguna,
Where time stopped in spring
And houses called off the hammering
Of the modern masons
And the modern artisans
Who were tiring time out –

In Belaguna, in Belaguna,
Time stopped in middle life and in May.
But the laughter of the monks of Mount Dondon
Went on musically instead.

The ten immortals not ghostly:
Brother Joseph, Athanasius, Gregory....
And the lovely Lady in the tower
Higher than the boughs, higher than the vine,
Up ninety-nine patient stairs,
Safe from these holies,
Safe for these holies,
Lying in the blessed bower
Of the merry monastery.

Desolate the Black River around Belaguna flows.
And peace eternal to the wanderer who crosses over.
And woe to the foot that flees
The breathless flower, the unfallen leaf,
The psalm of our lovely Lady of the Bower
In the rosy mouths of the monks of Dondon.

Nine pounds of bread, nine pints of wine –
God's careful coffers rationed no more than this.
How is the lovely Lady fed?
Nine bits, nine sips
Of nine pounds, nine pints,
Make a tenth of each.

Year after year,
Bead upon bead,
Stair after stair,
And a true heart under each scapular –
Oh, unwise holies, oh wise unholies,
Who vowed a chaste life
But never a chaste eternity!

In their only heaven, in Belaguna –
How came the lovely Lady there?
Not a monk knows, not a monk cares.
Who asked the Lady in his prayers?
Not a monk remembers the sweet supplication.
But they believe God hears.

And over and over again at their vespers
They chide God a little for His weakness,
They praise God largely for His goodness.

Each monk of God
Is the Dean of our Lady.
Each evening sets upon a Judgement Day
Not of rags and wrath but love.
Love's light penitences star the night,
The long, long night of the Sacred Lady
Of the lofty Bower
Of the lonely monastery.

In the confessional of the heart,
In the rhapsodic echo of prayer,
She is an ascertainable death,
She abides just above the air
And betrays them daily back to earth,
Who is the one of nine
The tenth of nine
And their eternal covenant.

How her magic came,
How their delight
Slipped from the sleeves of their prestidigitating night –
So wonder all the libidinous human hells
Swept sadly by Belaguna, by old Dondon,
Where God is the revelation
Of one merciful Lady in nine loves
And the fixed infinity
Of nine worshippers
In one beloved,
In one fair form.

Biography

You were born
    (I planted a tulip tree in my garden.)

You bloomed.
    (The cups of my flowers
    Were too frail for the dew.
    Each night I filled them
    With a tawny wine.
    Each morning
    They were too frail for the dew.)

You faded.
    (The wind stooped over my garden
    And gathered the broken petals
    Of my flowers.)

You died.
    (I have cut down my tree
    And made of it
    A staff of white poplar
    For my memory to lean upon.)

To-morrow I shall begin another story.
(To-morrow I shall plant another tree.)

Bring Me Your Passion

    Bring me your passion
    If it is turbid,
    For I am clear-eyed
    And will discover
    Perilous bottoms,
    Quivering sea flowers.
    I will behold you,
    I will illume you
    Till you are filtered,
    Till you are crystal.

Bring me your passion
If it is sombre.
I will be silver
Bed for your torrent,
White through your darkness,
Still to your purling,
Silk to your ripple,
Rock to your waters
Till you are laughing,
Till you are limpid.

Brothers

The first denies his nature lives at all
And grins fulfillment backward from the wall
Of an abortive spite against a life
Foredoomed he is unwilling to midwife
Out of the womb of a convulsive fate
To death it is his humor to frustrate.

The second plants himself the grudging stake
That will delimit life to him and break
The hungry spirit of him that would claim
A wider land and brood a fuller fame.
He covets no new acre, content to be
Becalmed in this cramped mediocrity.

The ruthless third, exalted and devout,
Tears doors in time and lashes life far out
Into a petulance of paradise
That spurns eternally the sacrifice
Of an unfettered faith he spurs to find
Wings for charmed flights that leave himself behind.

These three are blooded brother brother brother
Though each disowns the temper of the other.
Life dies a different death in every son
But death must live alike in everyone.
A separate bride enbosomed in each brother
Yet tells them all the son of the same mother.

But Lies

Oh, I've never had much good of telling the truth.
Love laughed at me and disbelieved.
Too true my flattery
Breezed under the glassy morning,
Broke the day's blue transparency
Over my passionate prophecies.

Truth being but one,
A delicate child and changeling,
Dies sleepily and sweetly in my arms
After each play,
Adds a new grief to my mothering gray,
Is born cruelly out of me babe again.

But lies are like old gods immortal,
Give me no trouble,
Blow each a bubble
That boasts and breaks,
Asks no grave,
Has no soul to save.

Callers

They come in suave demureness Sunday afternoon
To knock upon my door.
I know it must be more
Than zealous friendliness that brings them here so soon
To give me smooth caress of trimly gaunted hand
And sip a pallid tea
The while they gaze at me
Behind a barricade of smiles and greetings bland.

They softly walk into God's House on Sunday night
With simpering of praise
And sickly glozing gaze
At God, who thus importuned, hastens from their sight

More bold than I, to make a haply silent feast
Of guestless solitude,
A Host divinely rude,
Leaving the grace of entertainment to a priest.

Calotte's Lady

She laughed at all her wounds since they were wounds
Of love. "What care have I, Calotte, for pain
If love's long cure surpass no pain at all?"
Love was another earth in which she sowed
His many malices and reaped not hate
In harvest but the tender wheaten grass
Of love's full granary. "Talk on and on,
Calotte. Your warring words go whizzing by
And I am listening safely here because
Fear is unworthy of a loving woman."
And he was far away. And he could come
No nearer to prostrate her mortally
Since she was ringed immortally around
With love and flamingly secured within
Her proper passion. She could even pity
His agony of being too much loved
Since she who loved too much had only joy
Of it, but joy he would not have for comfort,
It was so true and terrible to feel,
Unless he could be terrible and true.
She never knew where finally he fled.
"What care have I," she said, "for faithlessness?
If, reckoning the ways of love, I find
His lagging love was none of these, I laugh,
I love, I double love, I am enough."

Coming of Age

Bright moons the children's faces fall down
That year the countenance is born.
Knowledge stares up unfeatured. There is dawn,
Dawn and one sun dividing darkness
Into one day.
Such is the inheritance of light, O little ones.
Trample the shining medals and headless march
With many thoughts, unmasked to understanding.
The certain mind is sightless groping
Its vatic way.
But the hours are vulturous. Even a visage is
A carcass although contemplation fronts
A ghostly glass. Night is ahead behind.
Paves with moons glancing pitiful
Their aged eyes
After the skeletons in blindfold flight
From Jove's birds nesting in the hollow heads,
Feeding upon the swift clairvoyance
Of flesh translated into death
Before it dies.

Compromise

I am the sun of whatever day may be to-day.
Oh, earth of my wild radiance,
If I had beaten back the inner fire of me
And given it only the freedom of myself
Until the tinder expiated
In a few fierce days and nights
The fire's necessity and mine,
Now we had been but two cold planets,
Waiting for no to-morrow.

But I have freed the flame,
Sent out the light,
Admitted you at least
Into the guarded ring of my personal universe
And imposed on you these limits of life and time.

159

I am the sun of whatever day may be to-day,
Burning my private eternity,
Never setting, never setting,
Single star of an earth
That sets ever on me,
To whom I have abandoned
For the love of kin and company
All my days and nights,
All my morrows.

Dedication

That I might not be lonely
In this strict adventure,
Brothers for my brave body
Tramp toward the sepulture

Beside me and endure
By hardship manifoldly,
Keep my allegiance pure
And cry my legend boldly.

But multiplied ordeal
Of many tries the one.
My spirit would not deal
This agony alone

If I alone had gone
And uncorporeal
Passed painless earth's red zone
Into the empyreal;

Nor made a destined age
Of a chance pilgrimage.

Doubters

The world may guard me well
From what is not the world,
Warn me to keep its spell
Unless I would be hurled
Into another hell.

Yet when the spell hangs low
And I may face despair,
I wonder where they go
Who have the heart to dare
Defy the world and know

The things the world is not;
And if, forswearing earth
For a precarious lot,
They laugh out of their mirth
That it's a heaven they've got.

Drinking Song

I
Before the Bowl

The melancholy in us scolds
The more immortal air
And gay;
And heavily the body holds
The all too short despair
A day
And asks a year
And yet another here.

II
After the Bowl

Ah, there is something in the cup
That turns the sad side down
And lifts
The laughing face of this soul up
Upon a dimmer town
That drifts
In wanner air
Away to anywhere.

Epithalamium of a Nun

The Christ-embrace has fallen like a curse.
The sacrament uncoils the serpent kiss
That wets the wafer. Flesh to the bride
Speaks lips and the hoarse fangs hiss
The prophecies of vintages.

Look for the violation of the soul
Higher than Eden, and beyond the bough
Know where the vine creeps and a sin is:
The virgin to her vow
When wine is drink and drink is thirst.

Christ, to be gentle, allows that faith and love
Be one. Christ in the color of faun
Leans down, and heaven hangs enchanted
Over the brow of a nun
Strange in her marriage as a nymph,

A nymph to Polyphemus were in love
And raging to be found yet in a flight
Of fright that she is otherwise
Than fleeing the frenzied night
Of glory in a blinded sun.

The litany is silent how the bride
Has fury feline in her hands asleep,
The eyes crouched narrowing and high,
Precise to the angry leap
Up to the vine and Paradise.

A mystery stirs her doom. A face appears
Next hers, fallen from the branch unnatural
Upon the upright pillow of
Her horror and the tall
Cliff of barren dreams, of self-suspicion.

She muses recognition, praying a sign
In her averted passion to call shame
Out of hiding to caress the stranger.
But cruelly a name
Knifes the pallid, empty distances.

"Christ, Christ, where art thou? I am called to meet
A gaze in darkness and confront to-night
Love with its everlasting evil
Of joy. Shrivel my heart, blight
Holiness, if I know you not, and smile."

Evolution of a Creature
Through Several Faces

The Love Face

The skin creeps close inseparable as apple-peel.
Ruddy on the bough this ripe grimace
Is a whole tribe grinning the hypocrisy
Of eagerness. The generation of a kiss
Falls to the ground. Flop. Flop.
The flattened lips turn up
An enlightened ape flabby with two cheeks
Hanging inelastic. The race snaps recklessly in sex
Into lesion. Like pins and needles
All the electrons fly from the expression

Stinging into heredity. Then painless
The twists impersonate another stare
For under passion lay a wizard
Waiting the descent of man and weary
Of the slow smiling of procreation.

The Frown of Displeasure

There is to do but what the roaming bear
Growls bravo! over, head-down in the head,
Contemplating idleness, the blind pearl
Of bodyliness. The features paw content
And bury the white mouth in muddy flesh,
Deep into sea-bottom. The severed face
Lifts an embodiment of gull now
Flying wing to fire. Beast after beast
Flashes in the spasm of astounded sight,
Till out of the brutish epilepsy of self-delight
Breaks a slow demon puckering its pride
Into composure to describe a man
Marked with his madness to forget himself
With physiognomy sporting in the brain.

The Assumption of a Name

Now the flushed image enters on violence,
Uncages the tempestuous doves
And drinks at their sleek breasts
An iridescent baptism of kisses.
Plague wails a gentle malice in the cotes.
The haunted population hears
Famine in its sleep and sweats a fever
Awake in one face mustering
The cries of doves out of the blank mirror
Where the Holy Spirit speaks no name
But a precipitous agony of numbers.

God's Proxies

God yawned and threw a cushion at a saint
And all God's little angels flapped their wings
And plucked their harps for melodies until
God yawned again and bade them stop and said
The berries on their bushes had no taste
And called for Adam whom God loved much because
He was God's fool and had no purposes
But tears and laughter and no friend in heaven
But God and was God's only friend. No one
Could say from where he came. The angels and
The saints disclaimed his parenthood and blushed
That God should call him son, not knowing whether
The word was spoken for the truth or for the sake
Of pleasant scandal at a pious court.

So Adam sang and Adam's lips grew full
And redder yet with his bright song and God
Caressed his hair and listened with a fond
And tearful inattention, while one by one
The saints (God called those saints who were the aunts
And uncles of the angels, for angels had
No other relatives) and angels quit
God's presence with indignation tucked under
Their wings respectfully that God should keep
A merry, unbecoming company
With a mad fool who chanted all his dreams
To make a king's mad holiday, while God
Laughed thunderously, crying, "Louder, son!"
Until there was no saint or angel left
To mar that little hour when deity
Forgot itself and romped with its first son
And fool and poet.

                Thus Adam sang that day
Of an imagined place that he called earth
And little creatures that walked on it called men;
And many other things did Adam that day
Dream for a tale to make God laugh and cry
A happy little crazy while. Meantime
The saints and angels eavesdropping at the door
Vexed their white peace with dark distress that one

Should dare to fancy in a dream a place
That was not heaven. But God had found a cart,
Wing-wheeled and gold and harnessed to an ox
All silver-white to a blue-silver moon,
And Adam laughed to call himself that ox
And laughed to leap with God over a moon
(This was another dream of Adam's nights
That were unholy gossip for the angels),
Upsetting him on earth in a soft patch
Of gaiety and tearing back again
Through winds and words and dreams to heaven and home
Before God could be asked for explanations.

God listened and laughed (or went out riding, as
Young Adam said, in a gold, wing-wheeled cart).
"Things have droll differences on that earth.
I told you yesterday about the men
And women. Don't laugh so, God. (I think there is
A saint's ear at the keyhole.) And there are
Some things that cannot move or talk at all,
Planted in what moves less than their still selves.
I call them trees and flowers." God roared with joy
And said that some day he would change the saints
And angels to trees, making leaves of their prayers
And shadows of their piety, and cried
That planted angels couldn't follow him.
And Adam laughed at God's bold, impious joke
And went on singing of that earth that he
Had shaped for him and God, lining his thought
With patches cut from fancy's unrolled fabric.

God grew more wild and in his madness knew
A boisterous desire to hide his feet
In such a stream as Adam told him of;
And longed to touch a soil that did not sift
Like air upon itself, he who had walked
Forever on nothing; and wept for the delights
Of littleness and pain and death and wonder;
And nodded tiredly then on Adam's tale
And fell asleep. For God was not much used
To merriment, and words and tales and dreams
Were like an old wine poured to make him happy,
And happiness that wine's intoxication;

Nor used to travel, where heaven was everywhere.
This is why God grew weary in a cart,
A golden cart, and fell asleep and dreamed,
Perhaps, and went on traveling again.

God woke and stretched his arms and rubbed his eyes
Into remembering and called on Adam.
But Adam answered not and a young saint
That had not learned to pout and worry yet
Said Adam had gone off not long ago
Singing of what he called his and God's dream
And of an earth he had imagined once.
"I'll find them both," he cried (the young saint said),
"And teach my creatures of heaven till heaven becomes
Faith and belief and doubt and nothing at all
And earth my dream's devised reality."

God wept and filled a saint's lap with his tears
And beat his breast and said that sons and poets
Paid all their debts with young ingratitude.
The angels raised their arms and hid from horror
When God blamed Adam for traveling without him.

God has had many fools since Adam's time
And each he has called son, winking upon
That name to trouble saints and relatives
Of saints; and each has sung and dreamed for God,
Making God merry, making God sad, and built
A wing-wheeled chariot for chasing songs
And dreams and earths to actuality,
And in the end gone traveling without him.

God doesn't care now. He listens to their tales
And sheds a tear at parting in bereavement
And bears his saints and angels for a time,
Knowing that songs and earths and dreams that are
Chased to a distant life will kill his sons
(Or fools or poets) and that some day each will
Come home again for burial, creeping
With crumbled wings through heaven's back door to make
God glad for sons (or fools or poets) that do
His dreaming and traveling and dying for him.

167

Golden Plover

Little by little the love that went a golden plover away
Dwindled to a sun-speck
In the heaven I made too high and wide for it,
While the wind turned up the frosted under-green of leaves
And my own winter brought me warm coals of forgetfulness
To run upon and take for streets and grasses
And something to cobble the naked pavements of my necessity
    with.

But there's my thirsting tongue
While the feet race,
And here is a life to live
And a poison to drink every minute in prompt doses
Until next spring
When a golden plover will come back
And with no loss of time or tears
Find another new nest to comfort in.

Grieve, Women

Grieve, women, for the sorrows not your own.
Grieve that in grieving you pretend them,
That men reluctantly
Deliver them.

Claim all your rightful provinces of tears
Out to the very shore of trouble.
But clamor not after the sea:
It is possessed.

The unabated weeping is your hearth,
While men abroad are blinded
By instant toil to tears.
Weep well, see far.

And ask no further sorrows of your own,
Embark upon no private peril,
Abide, pray for and mourn
You know not what;

Not thus to bring men and their mysteries home.
Home is no heaven but a haven
Where men leave grieving women,
Return to angels.

Houses

The secret population of the houses
Is not content with secrecy.
The palaces of sorrow are exploded
And joy is gotten in the going out
And the abstract successes of the street.
Sorrow is started up again in going in
And sleep employs
The comfortable beds
In concrete recollection.

But night cannot repair the violation.
The doors fly open the next morning,
Sunrise betrays the trapped dreams to a light
And death to day out of sepulchral rooms
These hands had built for tombs,
These hearts mistook for homes.

I Had Such Purposes

When you said that my love was like a cloak
And that it was too worn for longer wearing,
I laughed and answered that I was still deft
For a new tailoring if you would wait.

But you went with your fashionable coin
And bought thin elegances that endured
A brief gentility and then decayed
And left you ragged and shivering. I had
Such purposes for punishment and smiled
For all your unsubstantial finery
And wept and rapturously patterned cloaks
That I might know for retribution's sake
How warmly I might have appareled you....

I had such purposes for punishment....

I Have a Penance Too

Less than the air that is torn
Bloodlessly and invisibly
When the wind is furious
To rage among the calms
So fierce and foolishly,

Do I deplore how your blows struck
Unfortunate but blameless
Against my stoic side.
For of a mutual befalling
Quarrel came and following
Love and the double challenge.

I have a penance, too,
And you a pain of every sufferance
Bridled under the proud rein
Of my cruel intolerance.
Less than the air did I defend me.
More than the wind were you
Bruised among the calms,
Beaten upon the quiet currents
That never struggled but stood
Beauty like a smile
Unconquerable up to battle.

In Reverence

Her faith was a pope
Who went riding in a golden coach.
And she was bold enough
To ride beside him
As if she were his young and bonny bride.
Trot, trot, trot.
She sped the horses,
Forgetting quite
It was a staid old pope who rode beside her.
He held his sides and gasped:
Remember, dear, my age and dignity!

Trot, trot, trot.
Ho, you there trudging at the hill! she cried.
Come in and ride,
There's room inside upon his lap.
He said they'd wreck the coach
And crush his pride
Beneath them.
But she was elfin-spirited
And piled them in hilariously until
The horses slipped and all
Went rolling blithely down the hill.

She found him sitting in the grass
Where he had been dismounted all agape
With convulsive austerity
Sweating from his brow.
Well, well, she said,
And patted him maternally.
You're getting old, I'm afraid
I'll have to leave you home hereafter
When I go riding out.

Trot, trot, trot.
She galops now more jauntily than ever
In a dilapidated coach
That brims with giddy, supercilious company.
Why do you keep that seat beside you
Always empty? they demand.

171

Oh that, she says, is to
The outraged memory of
A fallen pope.

Joravaly

In the town of Joravaly
Two tribes hold their hands behind their backs,
The wicked never seeing over the high shoulders of the good,
The good twisting not a crooked glance
Around the haughty hips
Where irresponsible hands chuckle through skin
And hum on their finger-nails
Songs they know nothing about,
Songs that the good would throttle in their mouths,
Since ignorance is wisdom's sin
And sin is innocence.

The good hands hide.
The wicked hands hide but trill their tips.
Only the eyes come out,
Climb their tears to the same heaven
Where laughter and gravity are the same virtue
And the same sin.

Oh Joravaly, Joravaly,
Where to-morrow is blind
And to-day recks in unopened mouths –
Half the hands here are chopped at the first joint,
But the others trickle over the pianos of the past
And tinkle all the bad examples that make
Music and wicked men consolable
And good men bad.

Jugglers

What?
Is this the world in your hands,
Tossed bit by bit toward nothing,
Falling to floor,
Bouncing to being,
Tricked together
In fair weather,
Tied up with winds?

Open your eyes.
What have the hands to play with?
Close your eyes
Only the hands can see what the hands do.
The hands are blind.

Close your eyes
Lest they grope in the felt dark
And touch with the false fingers of sight
What the hands alone may behold.

Why?
Reason ties your hands,
Steps out like a new pupil
To practice clumsily with tidbits
Only the hands can put together
Into what they were.

Why? Why?

There are no ears.
There are no lips.
The deaf walk with the dumb.
Reason companions with a wraith unborn.

Oh the hands hear neither
But idle not,
Plucking the world preciously
As the fruit of a tree of one blooming,
Final and frangible
For a precarious juggling.

The hands live.

How.
Visible how.
How sees.
How hears.
How speaks.
How breathes and warms the hands.
How is the life.
Life is a mannered grace of moving.

What?
God knows.

Who?
Let death answer.

How?
Ah!

How beats on the hollow hands
(The rest of the body is still)
And drums out time.

Juggle, juggle,
Count, catch,
Toss, stitch,
The infinite mesh.

What is it?
Why is it?
The Great Nobody knows.

The way of it?

Hands!
Zealots of agony,
Exquisite, unendurable.

Lady of All Creation

Lady of all creation and perverse,
Dressed as a drab, the sacrificial inverse
Of all the beauty of the universe:

Having to choose between the act and state,
Why should you rather labor and create
Than be the quiet unregenerate

Of being? Have you not a smile to show,
Who must creep out of sight and creep so low
That sight may be a heavenly thing to know?

We cannot find you in your fair device.
This place is like a godless paradise,
Fade as a wine unseasoned of a spice.

Appear! Be fair! and we who are the doing
Of your dark self-denial won't be ruing
The end of all our worlds beyond renewing,

If you rise from our ruin enchantedly
The loveliness you meant our share to be
And let us live in you invisibly.

Last Women

Still, still,
Red tongues of desire
Lipped with an old demand,
Laughing and crying in the flesh
To win us variously,
Pleading in the deep places secret with passion.

Still, oh still.
The last child lies with the last mother.

Oh, magnificent extremity,
To be women and yet warriors against to-morrow,
Enemies and enemies.

Silent, whatever babes lie longing in the seed.
Choked in the stopped throat,
The wail of ages
Doomed in our contradictory denial

Of all the dear, terrible, womanly things in us
To ages of death.

Now, delight the end with indifference!
Sister us with the childless skies
And show our breasts
That will never spill for a child
Merrily from the broad hills with mother-pride
And wickedly at night to the star-nippled skies,
Daft with a new joy to be fair and futile
In the dusk of living that lasted long enough.

Now, gather as many flowers as women may
Who leave no children to gather the rest of them,
And heap them wastefully on our murdered men.

Still, voices, still.

Life Is A Thing...

Life is a thing somebody gave to me
To keep and have the use of for the while
I made a place for it in me. And long
I have forgotten the inconvenience that
Life put me to and loved the company
Of griefs I had not had without it there,
It was so fair and unbelievable
When first, half-charitably, I induced
This body to be affable to it.
Childhood contrived a playful peace for them.

In youth the two fell out and both began
The desperate revolt that could but end
In some mad sufferance of each for each.
And now my trust comes to its promised term
And someone's here again to take life back
And mark with what hospitable regard
It has been entertained these many years,
I have no grave apology to make
That what was unbelievable and fair
When it was new and left with me to keep
Should be returned so broken and pitiful
With all the uses that I made of it;
Unless, perhaps, remembering in turn
What I was like myself in the beginning,
As life goes out, an uninvited guest,
It give me some extravagant excuse
For all the uses that it made of me.

Named

Dance it was and no one dancing,
Cool fire and full spirit,
Pure performing without pitying
Self of flaming feet,
Heart of heat.

Air imbibed it. It was air.
Yellow flushed when was sun.
No name bespoken, only fair
Played a light with light,
Both in fright.

Man on man went up to see,
Saying, woman must be here,
Such delight cannot be
Unlovable or needless of
Name and love.

Man on man went up to see.
Came but one woman down
Nighttime, breathing heavily
Love like a name in her,
Too dark to stir.

Ode to The Steel Throats

The prophetic throats were gold.
They were gold in other days as they can no more be.
The fire is less melic, it is monstrous.
We need steel.
It is smooth, does not melt, it is made, is not mined.
Cool slips the fire like a spring from the lips
To a breath of sulphur.
The hearts alone are hoarse and have tears.
The throats are brave and will not break.
They are steel.
They are steel yet a color close to silver,
More blue and sombre.
The voices in a rainbow-span
Strike lightning close to the strong sun.
We have the sun nearer now,
In our throats even.
It may boil like sluggish lava
In a slow thunder.
The girders fulminate, they do not fall.
They are tucked in the throats
Tight and tender each as a violin
Is pressed under a chin.
They are steel.
Are they to love indurate as to fire?
Can the brass lips kiss?
They can kiss but the oracles
Flame up from Osiris to quiet Isis
Through the steel throats mysterious
To the woman gentle in the sacred dewlaps:
The word of love is death.

She takes no kiss.
She hears and hears no more.
The passion in the prophecy will end.

There will be an end of prophecy
As an end of love,
As an end of gold.
But steel shall still gleam
When the fire is frozen.
As well as fire, it can bear cold
And the brass lips be flesh to ice,
Be warm and waking to the frost-bound sleep
And chattering to speak.
There is sleep silent in all waking.
There is much waking in the chillest sleep.
It is a chance of chaos which shall scream
Nightmare, nightmare, and go mad with dream.
The throats are steel. They will not choke
Or close to terror clutching in a whisper
When the tongues hang leather
Wanting song like water.
They will not sing.
But they will say a thing
Needful, they will say:
"Nightmare is over.
We are not in the new day.
But the new day does not sing.
It is naked, it is golden.
The long throats and the wise mouths are gone.
God is the quiet. All is good now.
All is done.
Steel only stays, is faithful to the dead bone.
A privacy of speech shines in the silence,
A tremor sometimes in the might of girders
Runs like blood,
And the golden quiet bows its head,
Yields to the bright darkness that is backward
And tarnishes with tears
As if it understood
Or loved."

Reclamation

Shall her face be down, shall her eyes shine
Under the purple frost now toward the sun
Through the innumerable depths like a vine
Into the light, and lower lower shall her soul
Be womanly, be alone, address no man,
But serve herself?

She knew so outwardly. Her head bent perfectly
To her babes, she saw them well.
She was not blind. She beheld the truth
Confronting her to be caressed,
Needing love, or it might be sad.

Be her lips at last averted and her heart still
And the truth fully sorrowful
In her seamed eyes. She will not weep.
She will not see.
She will have much to think upon.

Though the door behind is open, she will return
In her better understanding but to close it,
To do nothing over, it was well enough.
She will not look back. She has greatness
In her second wisdom, in her death.
She had goodness
In her first.

Her life was quiet and the listening.
Now she cannot hear, she is mad.
She can move, she can sing.
Nothing can thwart her fright of rest.
Bravery has no babes here. She is
Required to be only proud, the revelation is
Her self-inheritance in the voice in travel
To itself known silent, for she does not hear.
She sings, it is not sung from any height.
It is buried and released to the light.
The light takes over what is swift enough
If it renounces,
If it does not stop for kisses,

If it flies alone through the dark
To reach the soul in the sun
And loves like a true woman
The hush of its own wisdom virginal
In death, the second self-denial.

Speaking in Me

The whispering you mark in me
Back of my still mouth
As of a tongue unnaturally
Stirring in a sound-drouth,

It is God speaking in me.
Remember I had him not as a father
And sire unalterably
But sworn as a brother.

And as such brothers there are
Words more than acts between us
And more mumbling than war,
Nothing more heinous

Than the grinding hate
Of two living close in a crowded house
Built to one inmate
And a mouse.

The argument behind the door
Shuffles and scratches privately
Upon the lacerated floor
That bears us up to disagree.

But one mouth will not report us both
Of the bicker and whisper,
So I take the quiet myself, very loth
To chatter me charitable my brother's keeper.

Summons

Come to me, man of my death –
Is it not death, what I am not,
The immanences not yet mine,
To be unbled with love?
I am a hollow without hunger.
Fate asks not to be fed but filled.
The end will be an end.
Stop up the narrow cyst
Most nothing when most provided.
The embrace imbibes us bodily.
Only the clasp and quiet stay
As death. Death must be something,
To have been made of us.

How impossible is abandoning;
Love is the lightest call,
But irresistable as death is.
The cruel internal I perceive
Under any mask. Beauty is a guise.
But destiny and the open flesh
Are more dire than beautiful.
I have a hound out that smells blood
In the whitest skin. I have a heart
Bleeding me hollow.
I can detect you as scent the dark,
With my eyes closed, truly.
Or, though my fingers turn in on me,
The thought of your thin face will be
Deep with the idea of your body.
Love is sure, life is more easily fled.
For life is only one in every one
And can escape itself without pursuit or heed.
Love is a place of numbers, where the conscience doubles.
It is the time, whenever it is the call.
Say no more it is not much,
No mystery unless we waste words on it,
Sob afterwards when we should be still,
Go on as ghosts when death is livelier,
Though strange, without a language,
And not unhappy, since there are no tongues.

The Call

I have lived too tirelessly,
I shall have to ask for rest.
I have loved too wildly,
I shall have to ask for death.

Will death wake me like the morning?
Will death call me to arise?
Surely I'll never answer,
But only bury deeper these sunken eyes.

The City

The city was not built of stones
But of five million broken bones.
Nobody knows how it began,
But first there must have been a man.
Too skilfully the artifices of the Avenue
Plunder the immolated skeletons of flesh and blood,
Provide a more decisive beauty in the form of silk –
Jointed, pointed,
Toughened, roughened,
The flesh devoured,
The sweet blood soured.
Upon five million faces falls a single countenance.
A public pact of concrete indivisibility
Destroys the numbers that there might have been to count and kiss.
Behold the well-paved pit.
No men grow out of it,
But it grows out of them,
Rests on a mangled stem.
The purpose to inspire a simpler life in these would be
Preposterous. Their skin stopped letting air in long ago
And now sensation is a superstition of the soul.
The furnaces forbid the chimney-smoke
To trail a spark or yet invoke
The higher fags to break the files
Of mouths that haggle over smiles.

What work are they about that has a new price every hour
And who will bid for it and blend the callous craftsmanship
With some use in the dusk to bear a new dawn out of it?
    Will ever one among them rise
    To break the million buckling ties
    And buy the steel eternity
    Bracing their bones where flesh should be?
And the new day would come. Flesh would creep back to warm
            the marrow.
The dead alive would be the living who know how to die
If but one man could see death is the price of anything.
    The city will be built of stones,
    Not of five million broken bones
    When there will be a man to cry
    That lifeless are who do not die,
    That living men do not belong
    In places that can last so long.
    Ah, but the city must be curst
    Since every last man is the first.

The Dawn of Darkness

I remember the first morning.
The mists of prevision mock me,
My flesh recalls reluctantly
The first far thrust of being.

The deep dust claims me first.
Before I can escape
The hollow heart of life will gape,
Bled white to death, uncurst.

Life lifted up her head: death was life's primal dawn.
Death will be now the dawn of men
As life lays down her head again,
Flings back the wakened spawn

To sleep and the slow mist from which we came.
Death surely is the dawn of destruction,
Yet surely was the inspired chaos of creation.
Life greets. Life says farewell. It is the same.

Dawn brims the day.
Levels to dawn once more.
Life is death's day and surplus store,
Returns the old way....

I look toward the first morning
From the long day and night.
Strained through life's tearful light
Comes death's bright dark and end of dying.

The Dead Know Nothing Now

The dead know nothing now.
Wisdom went abashed
Before the bright inquisitor,
Shadowless and throned and humble
Upon the living pride
That its pride knew only.

And they were winged and webbed,
Something each one had
To tell him truths that rot with him.
Envy starts afresh with every birth
Again and jealousy
Learns the last revenge

Of knowing ever nothing.
Flesh too much ennobled
By being forgotten in mockery,
Persecuted saintly by
Love and delight that had
Elsewhere fuller grown –

You need not fear the rest.
Death will only take
The little you never hoped or had.
Dark is the earth discoverable,
But heaven dazzled where
Mystery slumbers in bones.

The Defense

Of the Public Prosecutor
You might whimsically say that
He was like an elephant with
His proboscis for the law. Yet
He was strangely expeditious
For an elephant. One, two, three!
One, and you are nimbly tossed, and
Two, and you are snugly wrapped, you
Are a snail and he's your shell. Now
Three, pfiff, and a mighty blast, an
Elephantine blast (but do you
Happen to remember fondly
Those bright paper snakes you blew in
When you were a little boy, and
How they shot out virulently).
Oh – where are you? He has such a
Pretty aim for prison houses!

How he grudged that man Sylvester
His half-lighted aureole of
Self-denunciation, saying
That he stole his children's hour
From his day and bonbons from his
Candy bag and that he was a
Fatuous charlatan with pity
For his quackery. But those who
Heard Sylvester said that there was
So much artlessness in what he
Candidly confessed that he was
More the madman than the blackguard.

186

And he proved his crime so suavely
That the Public Prosecutor
Shook his hand when he was done and
Rapturously called him colleague:

"Simon Grimm and I were friends and
Ours was such a friendship as may
Come unconsciously to trees that
Grow so long beside each other,
That they'd only know what kind of
Friends they were if one were felled and
Carried off. When we were children,
We would gravely watch our eyes. When
We were men we saw a little
More than what might be in eyes, not
Transcendentally, but through slow
Plucking of the jejune gardens
That grew up to block the pathways
Of the houses that we lived in.
Soft-affectioned men we were not,
But our presences were goads and
Not caresses to each other.
Simon would come swaggering toward me,
Impudently shuffling, crying,
'Hi there, now, Sylvester, bet you
It won't rain to-day.' The story's
There. There wasn't anything that
We two had not slyly bet on.
We would follow some poor dog that
Waddled wistfully ahead and
Bet against each other on how
Far that dog would go before he'd
Wag his tail. Or if there didn't
Seem to be a single thing for
Us to bet on, we would bet on
How long it would be before we
Had something that we could bet on.

"One night, having waked and bet on
Houses, fireflies and toads, he
Took to wondering at the sky and
Said, 'Sylvester, see that star there

Bubbling from the brimming Dipper?
Must be far away, I reckon.
Yet it has a shrewd eye for me,
Narrowed as my Mary's is when
I come sliding in the doorway
On the other slope of midnight.'
And I always shall remember
How his eyes were wisely wrinkled,
Crafty as two stars they flickered.
'Sylvester,' he said, 'don't you know
People who have eyes that you would
Give an age of sight to look in
For a moment? I'd be willing
To give all that two dull old eyes
Could give to a blazing vision,
For the power to climb the sunset
And to peer inquisitively
In that eye so quizzically
Cocked at me. Sylvester,' said he
With an eerie humor that I
Counted for a night-time whimsey,
'Bet you I can bring me nearer
To that star than could ever
Come to canniness if God were
To make you ten times as canny
As you are.' That was his way of
Chaffing me, not seriously,
But as you will oftentime see
Mothers bantering with their young ones,
Grave as generals. I gently
Humored him as if I really
Were a cunning-headed youngster.

"After that they told me Simon
Took to scaling houses, though he
Never let me see him at it.
Only he would eye me sharply
As that evil planet of his,
Saying, 'Well, Sylvester, tell me,
How much nearer are you, brother,
To that star to-day?' He must have
Climbed each house in Sanahekan

And then lessoned with the chipmunks
Slyly for a nimble season
To have grown so lithe for steeples,
Yet not lithe enough for Simon
Was picked up one morning with a
Futile gentleness at the foot of
Saint James' Tower, as if he had
Rashly dared to play the gadfly
On its back. They managed somehow
To devise a sort of Simon
From the Simon that had once been.
But they had a feeble pattern
Of himself for modeling, and
When they pieced him all together
Neatly as a marionette, he
Was no more than that, for they had
Lost the inconsiderable link that
Might have made poor Simon walk, and
There was no Pygmalion's prayer for
His transfiguration. So he
Lay upon his back and whimpered
Pettishly for that one step that
Would have spanned the highest reach of
Sanahekan, for he figured
I could never climb up nearer
To his star than that, and knowing
Of the two of us which one was
Likeliest to crown a quarrel
With a pertinacious word, he
Had been unconditionally
Sure that I would never venture
Near as that to consummate my
Most importunate desire. But
Yet he lay and wept and chafed on
What he called his unfulfillment
Like a bird who sits repining
On an empty nest. And Simon
Now would not believe me when I
Told him that the bet was his and
That I'd never climb that tower
After him. But finally, I
Came to see, as on a sudden

You will find a gracile woman
In the moon where you have always
Watched a burly man, how I might
Help poor Simon win his wager
Irretrievably. Well, you may
Call it wilful murder with your
Untaught way of garbling labels.
So I hope that God will call it
Up there in his heaven with Simon.
Then when I am hanged next week, I'll
Know that I'll find Simon nearer
To that star than I could ever
Come were I to pass the fire of
Truth on God's next day of judgement."

The Door Ajar

When one spring will be shabbier than the last
In the most shiftless rain of all,
Call out of their more steady plane and past
The unimaginable men,
I know they are.

The door ajar
Between two rooms, two realms,
Will widen as they come and claim the end
Not in our name but theirs
And, if they can, by being us, forfend
The further and unmitigable sin
We dared in wondering, as we went,
What men, but for ourselves, we might have been.

The End

I live to wait.
I wait to live.
Life is the only end
That has my careful creed.

Nothing I do
All to aspire.
Astonishment
Of hope not of
Accomplishment
Is my last wonder.

What spring can share
With me I spurn for
The purer bare
Of prouder winter
That is no season
But fruitless self.

Thus I adjure
The roads that rip into the sky,
Return and mend the mark,
Intrust the travel to the dark
Wending of thought.
The end is then
The confessor of the start,
Even as death's quiet comfort,
Proof of my hopeless heart.

The Fourth Estate

The newspaper reports people as usual.
The paper double of fleshliness
Continues to keep life fashionable
And flatter the uncertain original.
We read with faith, rubbing the fictive lamp,
And soon the gossiped genii appear

Out of the broad page, and by report
We know ourselves, are quieted
By the printed pictures of us hung
Upon a flimsy wall.

And the sheet circulates perhaps beyond
The private limits of earthly rumor.
And the advertisement is of an active portrait
That serves a quiet model,
Pleads a good place in the remote gallery,
Secures the creature the dusty immortality
Of a fantastic memorandum
In a forgotten file.

The Gropers

The flowers are out to feel.
The blind flowers are fingering for the vesper:
First a bug then the wind then a bird then the wind,
All asleep, all asleep....

Now the stroke is grazing lighter:
Something jealous, something watchful,
Men and men....

Here they rest,
Feel no further for the vesper.
Men are closer,
Pluck more quickly....

The Haunt

Content the conscience with a moon of blindness
When the black fear rises out of chaos
And a lamp would burn too brave.
The beams blare in a hush cloudless.
The haunt is on.
"Where can we be?
Where can we be?"

We came.
Was there a place?
Is the cry close to the tongue and a blister
Or a howl in hell, where we once were?
The night knows nothing but a moon,
Sees terror with a stark eye.
It is the shuddering mind
Of ancient instinct wakening,
Grown wise remembering,
That paces the dark island to the brink
And knows by the warm wane on the lids
Brightness is everywhere but here.

Heaven and hell wreathe us from the same fire
With ghosts or angels
As our brows beam light.

The Hills

The hills would be lovelier afire.
Surely when the early light takes them for flesh,
Surely they quiver and think of love
Their way recessionally into hiding,
Face-down against the morning.
Light is up-looking.
How can the hills be happy, grieving down?

This is earth, fallen into gulfs,
Fast and safe.
The hills billow but are still.
The currents run a quiet serpentine,
And earth is aqueous of the fire it is not,
And the dust is false, only fear.

Light has another law.
The hills heave and dare
Turn and unveil, be aware
Darkly of light and rise
When they can rise black
In the charred pillars of a passion
That never burned but sank
Where there was no water
Or a flame to drench.

The House

The house arose and how I never knew.
But my restless hands would never let me finish it.
I never saw the last light lit
Nor learned how the marigolds grew.

For they said because of Calman
I'd be worse than dead
Living in my lonely house,
Sleeping in my satin bed.

I had treated with the local birds
To sugar the dawn.
The spiders had already begun
To dimple my new garden pool.
Spring breathed up the lawn
And smothered my Calman under it.

I don't remember what Calman did
That made me kill him
And build my house
And bury him in back of it.

(For how else could I be close to my only lover,
With no chance of another?)

Strangers have my house now,
Strangers have my garden.
I think of the birds hopping over Calman
And I'm lonelier than dead
And curse me for minding what the neighbors said.

The King of Love
(To Pedants and Puritans)

The King of Love had nothing left but love.
His realm was doubted and his parentage
Impugned because of certain patches in
His moldered cloak.
      The King of Love could not explain
      How he was King,
      How he had come by his terrain
      And governing.
The bastard would not own an ancestor,
Had not a mother even to recall,
Or else was promised to protect her name
From scurrile folk.
      The silent King resigned his throne,
      And whipped his cloak
      About him, went away alone
      Before they spoke.
The rule of Love was over and the trance
Of peace too tragic, torn and uncomposed.
Love had unlived himself and lay again
Unborn in hell,
      The dream of an unmentioned Fair,
      Lucifer's bride,
      The other partner of the pair
      That side by side
Dared venture out of heaven's harbored cold
Into the open and original fire
That warmed an earth and withered what grew on it
Too long and well.

195

For these the devil and his bride
Begot a child
To be their King of Pity and guide
Out of the wild
And waste and simmering terrene
Into a place
Far from the scarred and smoky scene,
The little space
Of dispensation, heaven, that
They now refuse,
To learn Love's ancient habitat
And surely lose,
To know his name, Love's heritage
Of love, and hers
Who bore him for a thankless age,
And Lucifer's.

The Liar

I deny my moods.
I escape them.
I prove our separate nothingness.

I deprive my moods of their limbs and lips.
I deprive my moods of their mechanism.
For anatomy is the mechanism of my own soul.

I deny anatomy.
It is the mood of my soul.
My soul is the mood of myself.
Myself is the microcosm of the Liar.

I shall seek the Liar.
I shall recognize him by his moods,
Banners flying in the wind of his Temperament –
Myself a loose banner
Liberated in the accident of a storm.

I shall prove my separateness.
I shall oblige him to deny
The little lies of his moods.

So will he accomplish my destruction
And discover his own.

I deny my moods.
I cry the truth of disintegration.

But the Liar will not hear me.
But he stops his ears
With the breezes of a new mood.

To be nothing and yet exist!
Liar! Liar!
Bind me again to my staff!
I affirm my moods.

The Quiet Echo

To whomever our travail will seem
Not so terrible
That patience for another hour
Is an impossible
Prayerfulness of life and pride.

To him shall be, though but a god
Of false priority,
The making of us many times over
For such agony
As leaves us voice to ask it over.

Of our most cruel endurances thus
Cries out the prayer
Mightiest to reach the end
Of crying where
Starts back the quiet echo from god.

To a Cautious Friend

Foresight may mask
As the prophetic faith only until
I need, I ask.
Then reason parts around you to fulfill
The friend I lose or win
As you go out, come in.

It never shall be I
Or anyone who heard the tale from me
To say which did you, why.
Love touched my eyes in time just not to see,
And better, before I begged a groat,
Love touched my throat.

To a Gem

I had been looking forever
For a stone like this,
And never did forever
Find an end as fair as that I gave her,
Pinning this dim old stone between my breasts
To answer the long cry of my lonely bosom
And kiss away the dark print
Of a brooding emptiness.

Chip of some ore you have forgotten
With all the other hearts you lay upon,
I had lived and waited
Unlighted here, unadorned,
Keeping this place bare and virginal
Not for one like you
But for you.

Peace to us both now
In our brief together,
Caught in our proper destiny against each other.
But remember, oh remember,

198

Hence a shift of years
As you blaze and glow and darken
Over some other tremble of breath and flesh,
How you once rested on me where we met
And contributed to each other
And ever exchanged our separate charms
Back and forth over the wistful barter
Of all the differences in us.

Perhaps one day –
Who sees the skeleton's garb
Or knows in what tokens the dead go dressed? –
I shall parade proudly among my ruins,
Recalling only that habit of my bones
That bore you on me;

And forbear to look a moment –
Lest I disturb what might be burning for a moment there
Before I turn to look and grin again....

Perhaps one day
I shall remember too.

To I————

Your voice more than any song a song,
Your feet quiet so aquiver,
You will not dream – sleep is too long,
You will run with a river
In your heart lie a courser
Charged with a flood –
Fast feet, fast blood.

Has the race no mate, does it not move?
Do you sorrow: I went too slow?
Think, dear, there is more than love,
More than the earth to go.
It is but alone
It can be flown.

Sing then toward where seems nothing,
Run where there lies no space.
The crowds cannot be anything
But each a foreign face
Whose eyes remind
How far it is behind.

IV

Addresses

Mother, you say,
My body came a mysterious way.
Mother, I know.
You need not tell me so.
My body will go.
But I have a soul to stay
That came in a simple way.
It is larger than my body.
It makes the world seem cloudy.
It is something like my dreams.
It is like my body's shadow.
Yet it does not follow it.
I don't learn more than worry of it.
It doesn't learn anything of me.
It has a face I cannot see.
It has a voice I cannot hear.
I don't know whether it's dread or dear
Or what it is singing
Or whether to me.
But mother, I know that we are we.
When beautiful blue falls down on me
So sky is all my eyes can see,
It is my soul kissing me.
Body is only a little boy
Bashfully wrapped up in a cloud.
Mother, when the boy grows proud,
Cloud and boy will be one.
Cloud and boy will be clear.
Mother, can this come next year?
Or will the little boy fall out,
Never be able to climb back,
Until he's old and married
Or dead and buried?
But mother, mother, this cannot be.
By then my cloud will have grown strange to me.

Father, I have begun to think.
Come and listen at my head.
It is frightful, like being dead
And having to hide
Everything in you that was once outside.
Father, can you look through me now
And see the world behind my brow?
Living in me like a house
And master in it to unlock
Every part of it with a shock
To the wild dark behind the door
Shut in with itself and full of fright
To touch its fingers or let any light
Intrude upon the anchorite?
Father, father, what could I do,
Crowded where was no room for two,
But one out alone?
Have I no shame to stand out of my body
Bare as a most beloved lady
Beside herself with love?
Tell me, how does it behoove
A thinking boy to place himself
Among his thoughts in his opposite world?
It is best to run away and hide
And be bold in everyone else's world
And lie face-up in hot fit
Of life on someone else's street,
Outside, outside.
Inside is in my own head dank
And dark and of me ghostly blank.
Forgotten and so self-afraid,
I'll have to shove my own spade
To splice the light into my skull
When the time comes for my burial.
And from my head and very high
I can climb deep into me to die.
Father, more needful than to have
A dark house is to have a darker grave.

Wife, wife, you are too much at my side.
Woman, your beautiful blinking eyes
Make me too much apologize
For what you do applaud
With such allowance, Maud,
Of love where the walls I build are weak.
Maud, you are too much at my side, and meek.
Make off before me to the desert.
Fly from the sand up with the sphinxes.
Think walls of me
Where walls cannot be.
I will not be tried by a woman,
Be beholden to praise for anyone,
Though I have raised a high house
And caught quail for my silly spouse
To feather and fry in proud sauce
To be silk in my jaws.
Praise is lodged tight, dear wife,
Not in your heart, how it heaves
When I enchant mortar, or grieves
When I have made the pots and eaves
Invisible in my sight and only your blind heart sees,
And no others, what I have set over trees;
Praise was first of me.
Before I knew, I came to be
Of an original applause and prophecy.
Get you into the desert, then, and to death
Straightway. Love will not hold your breath
A minute more than life,
Or my walls climb you into heaven, wife.
They were built to fall
And fall down far as they were tall
Until they reach the oracle
That from the first did trust
Me to my line and my self to the dust.

Child, what you do insanely criticize
With your mother's mute brain and my mute eyes,
Is not the speechlessness of the cows and crickets
Or the things too terrible in the thickets
To look out and smile. Though no lips seem to break,
The question throats a deep lake
And the still is neither dumb nor blind,
But laps the vision in your mind
In a tongue you do not recognize
Since it talks with quietly living out
The thought and live thoughts do not shout.
So hush, child, hush, and don't listen, look.
It is not speaking, it is a book.
The black and white are in your head.
The pictures and the blood are red.
But the narrow eyes squint
And goggle the universe into print.
Short-sightedness brings its own bulge close
To its spectacles. Error sees through error.
The perfect maladjustment of the mirror,
Child, child, is why you see,
Why you are the precise child of me
And your mother Maud whom I took
To make subject matter in the book
And some sense and day-time,
Lest too literary be the crime
Of creating you, and the theme
Implicit utterly in a dream
And I, the only supernatural sleeper,
Be awakened to be killed
For a dream too supernaturally fulfilled.

V

Outlive me, ghost, along my liveliest ways.
Plow upon the carpet's ribboning craze
Over the proud boards. They held me up,
Warped to the stellar pole, and eaked an arc
Rivaling Boreas sputtering the Banshee in the cold.

I pirouetted on the manifold
Spiral, toed my zenith
From the black plinth
Of Tallus, struck the halo of my arctic skull
With sparks. Follow the fragments of this animal
Into their martyrdom and let them coruscate,
My spirit, upon the ceiling above the deathless weight
That walks the soft floor bare and hollow.
Look from the quicksand inferno
Up to the beaded nebula
Signing aurora
And implore the horoscope, on sunken knees,
My resurrection sheds to the antipodes.

Ammon's Grief

"For which of your bloody deeds, Ammon,
Betray you now this secret grief?
Is it the thief remembering
The finger torn off with the ring?
Or the havoc you did last December
In the old lady's chamber?"

"Fool,
Do you think I would pet and pule
Over such a thing I did last Yule?"

"Ammon, has the Parson put hell
Like a pill down your gullet
And do you now feel the ashes in the flesh?"

"None of this, I'm as learned in hell as he.
I make it; he gives it a name.
I secure it; he spreads its fame."

"Is it a better bandit, Ammon,
Has won the devil's plaudit?
Is it a false accomplice
Has forfeited your hiding places?"

"None of this, friend, none of this."

"Then wherefore groan and drool, Ammon,
Over such a lucky life?"

"No more lucky is it, fool,
For I've wed me to a wife."

"Do you fear she'll thin your purse?"

"Friend, my purse can fatten fast."

"Do you fear she'll pray you good?"

"Friend, I fear she'll pray me worse,
Bring upon me bad-man's curse.
Bad-man's honor does but bless
A good-humored wickedness."

Another Kind of Bird

Another kind of bird:
It was not singing I heard,
It was not a screeching shadow
Nor the stinging croon of an arrow,
But the sipping up of a sea
As I, alone, drink tea,
Not loving it,
But thirsting for company.

I never saw it poise,
I knew it in a night,
I knew it as a noise,
Its faring was not flight.
But of the many things that it might be,
It might be most a bird.

Rain cannot tap away
The rhythm of its wrapt imbibing.
Wind cannot betray
The steady still of either wing.

I have no fear of its ever coming
To pluck out my moist heart
Or of hearing too early the humming
Of its devious dart.

Less abruptly does it sup
Of my ebbing blood
Filling up the flood,
Supplying the sea
To the last drop
That will drink and dry me up.

Not till then will it fly away with me.

Can Lips Be Laid Aside?

Can lips be laid aside
As they were pipes outplayed
And the voice at last quiet
Called the voice perfect?
It is a secret not for speaking.

Can the unfleshing of the face
Reveal the full regard,
The clouded dazzlingness
Garbled in the grimace?
There is no glancing on it.

Put the whole body by.
Uncaress it stonily.
It renounces the impossible love,
The hardy dedication,
For a shape of no embracing.

Then may the voice invalidated once
In the lips' employment
And the imprisoned image of the crooked mask
Array the splendor unperceivable,
The entire unappearing
It is false to sight with seeing,
Name with knowing,

Dallydilbaree

From the Fountain of Dallydilbaree
They had their loveliness, the ladies.
And modestly informed they were
Most intimately from afar, afar.
The source and spray were air before
The wind sipped and was consecrated
To blow around and around in pillaring whorls
Everywhere until everywhere girls
Grew delicately wisps and wreathings first
And flesh only as afterthought
And ladies next
And women last.

And as women bewailing
Beauty was a boon unbodily
Foamed windwise out of Dallydilbaree,
Fanned windwise back
After the interval of life
That is love in ladies.

The petulant prayers seeking the source,
The local breath betraying the essence
Large to the atmosphere again
And out of the air then into rain
Replenishing the far fountain,
Cannot spare the specific charms
Of Laura, Elinor or Kate
The incessant bubbling up of beauty
Gurgles and crowds to evaporate.

For ladies and love allow an end,
But the bottomless springs of Dallydilbaree
Are sunken through to the other side
Where ladies and liquids are compounded
Capriciously of nearly nothing
And sparkled up to quench and please
Men and other certainties
Unearthed here and hovering over
Dallydilbaree's brink. There many a lover
Sounding the evanescent silver
Thirsts his sad eyes down
The cavernous brown
Through to the blue
In which beauty must drown
Though bodies be buried.

If a Woman Should Be Messiah

If a woman should be Messiah
It might not be an impressive drama,
It would be but a slight event and unsignaled,
It could not but be beautiful.

Such a woman would surely say very little
Of morals and religion.
Such a woman would surely never travel
Or inspire a gospel.
She would live at peace shyly
With a local lake and on certain days
Intrude some nearly divine distress
Upon it, with a most feminine caress
As of weeping spotlessly over it
In tears no more wonderful
Than any other woman's.
She'd have no unnatural hungers,
No fewer lovers,
Do no evangelical tricks
With stones and sticks,
Even employ the innate art

211

To win the ordinary heart
Of an ordinary man,
As any wilful woman can.
And, as with any other woman,
Her self-confession would be kept
Close to her kerchief, under the pillow where she slept.
She might be adored of her household.
She could never deny them her faults.
She would pamper her private follies,
Talk too much of her dreams,
Pray to a personal God,
Deal unhistorically with facts,
Be sweet in marriage and motherhood.
Who'd be aware of her quiet work?
Who'd call her a savior or even a saint?
Who'd trouble her with a cross or a church?
No one would.

Jowl and Cowl

Fresh is the early sin at least
In the late age
And beautiful bare is the flesh of the sage
Despondent in his scornful cowl.
As the healthy hide of the bygone beast
That chucked his own jowl
But once after meat
And blinked his contemplation into sleep.

Only the immortal mind
Seems older
This year by another beauty,
Shivering colder
Out of covering, out of body,
Blowing to find
The golden early angels of the origins
That lay down lazily to sleep
And rose to weep
Chastisement with true eyes
Blinking forgotten wings.

And only the immortal mind
Will breathe fast to-morrow
And wilfully go
The lost way of its kind
While an empty cowl
Flaps mournfully to tatters
Beside a happy resurrected jowl
Doubling on a wakened angel.

Last Nuptials

A husband is for heaven,
Then ancient and God.
Timidly touch his silken straw beard, ladies,
And adore his autocratic infirmities,
Yourself no more in pitiless prime,
All blessed in permanent assembly,
None kissed in petty privacy,
No separate slippers for love has he
Than these lined so darlingly
With lamb's ringlets and frank upon
The public hearth as they should be.

Meanwhile in maidenhoods
On earth he does allow
Of little lovers and such invasions
As grace on guard may smile upon,
Since, in the exchange of hungers
And need retailed for need,
Hunger cannot hunger feed;
Only the amorous agility,
The skillful quality will rise
Of the tendernesses trained
In uncomposable agonies
Aspiring toward the sedate satisfaction,
In the heavenly household,
Of the balm of ecumenical benefaction.

So to me has been granted
Alastor and Leonidas
And three, to count a cousin, before
And three and three after,
Not including Alastor's brother
Who, with a cadet's closeness to his mother,
Pitied a woman in me
And helped me to flee
In his own way the night of the fierce fandango
When I stripped off my priceless costume
In the Weather-Vane Room
And revealed the secret of my left breast
To the half-horror and relief of the rest,
Except of the youth
To whom I later told the truth
About the indelible dye....

Whether after all this
(And the experience as well
Of the crossing of the Wrong Channel
In my best belongings
In answer to a death-bed summons
Forged by my foreign friends for fun)
I shall be willing to become a wife
On most reasonable rations
To the genial Spouse
And churn and chat in my corner
Of the gigantic cottage;
Or whether the indulged meretricious
Prejudices of the flesh
Will deem it more delicious
To enlist as a courtesan in hell
And so stain my lips rather than my hands
In preparing my Lord's pottage
And keep a light instead of a wholesome heart –

Ah, it is a secret I dare not impart,
I dare not even own.
If it is not permitted to plot alone
Though to no merriment or mischief
I can at least step off the bridge betwixt
Me and my morrow,

As many a woman and Mona Lisa
Abandoning her babes and assignations
With more sense than sorrow;
I can go crying in my peculiar way
And falling forever
In the line of the drunken tower at Pisa.

And falling forever
In the line of the drunken tower at Pisa,
We shall both crash together,
Shattering our secrets.
And it will never be known in heaven or hell
How my only pure impulse committed suicide
As, forecasting my eternal mate,
I lamented for one moment
An immortal spirit might not be celibate
Before the insatiable bride
In me espied
My Lord's sweet beard
And as of old wondered
How well a whistle could be heard
In heaven from a red distance
While my Lord God slumbered.

Love and a Lady

As were the old Chinese, cruel and dead
From contemplation upon death, so he
Seeking an escort to the open grave
Of resignation he had banked himself
Among life's miserable certainties
Like pain, like love – asking a human friend
Forever, Varla asked too little, too much.
All men must be misjudged through time's reprieve
Of judgement until faithlessness has chance
To enter in the promptly loyal heart;
And after time there is no judgement or
A need for anything, least for a friend,
Where loneness is immense companionship.

215

But Varla had a tongue and talk untalked
And craved an ear to trouble with his peace,
Carried a heart that wanted worry that
Was not its own and coveted a stage
Within another's soul he might enact
His favorite performances upon.
Out of the friendless gloom came not a friend
But something better, came a woman and
A friend in one, enclasped him in a love
He took only as part of his own light,
As friendliness, or as a flower to pluck
Benevolently, commended to his mood
Never the darker way, never along
The stoic roots of reticence to love,
The gallant soil that grows the flower but claims
The prizes for the flower alone. He knew.
Fear was the knowledge of her love for him.
He asked a closer, kindlier thing than love,
That lay over the brink of beauty, deep
And dangerous, unnamable, like death
In shadow, unlike death without a life
To live before it, to precipitate –
And after, what were tears, to be attained
So desperately? And there would be tears.
There would be death in any case. His need
Was not a fresh experience of life
But of an ease, but of an end of self,
A safe release, a sleep. But where was sleep
In love, that waked in uttermost the night
Of solitary secrecy, widened
The shy extent of the contented soul
Until to love a simple human meant
To be impossibly responsible
For all, and all to the last waiting keep
Of a ridiculous reliance of
Some outer, stronger universe in him?
"Oh no, no, no, dear lady, merely this:
A little reparation for the skimp
Of my own body to contain myself,
The violent implosion of the mind
Too full in an outwitted body, turned
An outward grace when given outwardly

216

As nature. I'll be shrewd in using you,
Like nature kindly in concealing it.
But let it not be love or it will be
All loves that ever were set loose to sweep
Across me like the greedy hounds of hell
After my speeding soul's immensity
That fades in fleeing like a timid hare,
Its life grown suddenly in the pursuit
Too precious, too appalling, yet a thing
Unalienable. Love knows no content.
Love sows and harvests of the soil and seed
At once. Will you refrain, dear lady, ask
What I can give away as alms and not
Invade my heart to hunt and trap my soul?

"Trust me, sweet Varla, the extent of what
Your confidence requires," she answered him.
"You'll never know from any sign from me
Whether it be a woman or a dog
That shares your privacy by keeping it
Close as an unsplit pea. Nor will I spy
Or scent upon the true taste of the fruit
Or let my mouth run sour in hope or hate
At having not. Stand me upon the side
Of your most bleeding sorrow and I'll be
The necessary nurse but never ask a kiss.
Or set me up to celebrate a joy
I must not have a part in – you shall see.
I know. I've been to Paris. I can make
Least love of most. What, Varla, is it not
Enough?" For Varla strained two anxious eyes
Upon her over-acquiescent smile.

"Woman, you are too willing to deal well
With me." "I do but wisely choose," she said,
"Between my love and my beloved, sir."
"Can you put love away so easily?"
He panted. "If you bid it, and why not?
What pool cannot be smooth when stirring stops?"
He stood perplexed. "What is it now?" she asked.
"This love," he said, "it is not difficult?"
"No, no, not very." "Child, speak further, tell me –"

Night

Light was always.
Night we cried for;
And with brightness
As for more light.
From the heavens flaming
Fell an understanding,
Fell the yellow fruits, the plums,
The skin in cloud-bloom,
The sweet meat splashing,
The rough pits puckering
The eyes to wrinkle,
Of a wryness, first taste of night.

In a busy mist the plum-wine
Was pressed and poured by frothy fingers
Singing swiftly in the filling
Of the bottles pursed,
Lipped up from thirst
Of open throats
That could not drink
Or swallow on the dark
While the sun stood still
Parching the song.

In a quenched and quiet dusk
When night was no more new,
The last storm broke in music
In the last bottle to be broken
And a drenched bird flew
Fruit odorous from the bubbling.
The wrinkled eyes followed him
Out of sight into a dream,
Into the orchard of the plums.

Then fell another understanding,
Fell a drift of feathers,
A death of yellow flight,
Down-fluttering of the forsaken light
That once had bloomed the lovely black
And given blindness drink
Until the eyes forgot.

What could be bright
In place of light?
Think of the night, the proud-plumed eyes
Opening peacock-wide to play
The hoarse pantomime of day.

Reunion

Only what has passed out the golden gates
May enter in.
When earth was fullest green
Out blew the least obedient gust
Eddying the long way down,
Alighting with a sudden body
In whichever town.
The sudden body
Was a lady.
She married Andy.
She bore three children.
No good for any of them it meant
The truth of her descent
Could scarcely compromise
With earthly exercise.

Only what has passed out the golden gates
May enter in.
Yet she bequeathed them
A special rhythm
She blew upon them
A certain accent
And she can claim them
When she has risen, a little later,
As she whirls hungrily along the barrier
Greeting hopefully
Each similar spirit entering
That may be,
Can she but recognize the melody,
The humming of
Her husband Andy

Or which of her three children?
Mandy?
Sandy?
Dandy?

The Dissolution of One

The judgement, the atonement,
Must all take place
In his scant buried body,
And heaven's grace.
Heaven isn't any place.

The punishment and pleasure
Undoing the firm
Prove the numerous nibbles
No different worm
But a different infirm.

This for a kind revision
Of a brute blow,
And another for a sudden sin
Not altered so.
Good is an unamended blow.

His self now all inherent,
Not of a scene,
Publicly in full private
Can own its spleen
Nibbling up the disguise of the scene.

The judgement, the atonement,
Now all take place
Anywhere and everywhere
In God's great embrace.
Only hell is a place.

The Quietest Song

What were birds made for,
To sing or sing about?
Is it a contest
And can you match
A tongue against a tree,
Music with melody?

Be judged better in your silences,
Vain songsters.
Night and a nest
Contrive a common peace,
A reverence and rendering
Of each to each.
The quietest song is sleep
Where self allows the strings and wings
The humble grace
Of dreaming other things.

The Victory

Before I had a plot and plan
And counterself and conflict,
When I was greater than a man
And not dust derelict,

There was a starry order
Where I flew freely
From border out to border,
Never free entirely,

But bound in an endearment
Born of the patient need
To keep from full abandonment
To the flower in the seed;

Until an alien evil
Split the sinless shell
And a gardening devil
Bloomed me into hell.

Growth belies the promised span
Of unadventured power.
War between the mind and man
Divides the seed and flower.

Victory will rest with heaven
When success is spelt
Out of fragments of destruction
Life to life has dealt.

Early hope and later failure
Will be friendly in the glory
Of the long and final grandeur
Telling both in one death's story.

V

Dimensions

Measure me for a burial
That my low stone may neatly say
In a precise, Euclidean way
How I am three-dimensional.

Yet can life be so thin and small?
Measure me in time. But time is strange
And still and knows no rule or change
But death and death is nothing at all.

Measure me by beauty.
But beauty is death's earliest name
For life, and life's first dying, a flame
That glimmers, an amaranth that will fade
And fade again in death's dim shade.

Measure me not by beauty, that fears strife.
For beauty makes peace with death, buying
Dishonor and eternal dying
That she may keep outliving life.

Measure me then by love – yet, no,
For I remember times when she
Sought her own measurements in me,
But fled, afraid I might foreshow
How broad I was myself and tall
And deep and many-measured, moving
My scale upon her and thus proving
That both of us were nothing at all.

Measure me by myself
And not by time or love or space
Or beauty. Give me this last grace:
That I may be on my low stone
A gage unto myself alone.
I would not have these old faiths fall
To prove that I was nothing at all.

A Pair

Those two had sewed themselves a dignity
From all the patches of failure they had cut
From the success of others. And their heads
Were high in an austerity of grief
For what they had not been. I cannot say
They loved, for they only lived
In profile to each other,
Looking on life as it were a relief
Against eternity. And when they spoke
Their voices left no echo for they pricked
The surface of silence lightly as a thought.
And oh! how cruelly neat their house! There were
No kindly folds in curtains, no idle chair
Pulled carelessly askew for gossiping,
But everything was crucified on walls.
Even the sun was a severity.
They never had a child, for it would be
A sign of some prosperity.
And had they yet, I'm sure it would have been
A shadow, for these two were
Ephemeral as two may be and live.
And I have come to know that all they have
Was all they could ever come upon
Even had they encompassed a success.

Adjustment

You thought our arms were too pertly
Akimbo for two chairs that were
As old as we. You said there was
Something obscenely gay in our
Perverse hilarity and took
Us to be sobered in the attic.

A gaffer and a gammer now,
You two, as blithe as yearlings you
Declare to all your little ones.
But they are arrogantly tender
For all your wistful liveliness
And superciliously bring
You shawls and slippers worrying
That their new furniture may be
Too spry for elderly repose.
They pried into the attic and
There found two chairs grudgingly sober
And said that they were quaint as those
For whom they brought them down, with their
Old arms akimbo in a worn
And bravely bolstered jollity.

The Lightning

The cold white lightning
Leaps like a ribbon of steel from its furnaces
And jag-saws the sky till it thunders with pain.
The cold white lightning is beautiful.

The long swift lightning
Mows down the little trees
And buries them in the rain.
The long swift lightning is beautiful.

The cruel bright lightning
Sharpens its flame on steeple stone
And rubs a spark from a little life
And puts the little spark out.
The cruel bright lightning is beautiful.

The City of Cold Women

THE SKY

The winged stars poise over the city,
Frozen by the breath of the cold women.
The moon is a frail defiance to the cold women,
Waning to a last chilled wisp.

What is more cool than the girlish dawn?
She peeps over the arched shoulder of the moon
And calls the sun like a frightened child.

What is more cruel than the sun to a frost?
But there is no whiteness
Like the whiteness of these women.
The sun labors at parting in fear-fraught anguish,
Knowing how her womb must yield the twilight
To the indifference of the cold women.

These are the heavens of the cold women,
Timorous and benumbed.

THE WIND

The wind shudders through the city,
Wrapped in the shawl of its swiftness.
Who but the cold women
Have fingers to tear quietly
The shawls of the chattering wind?

THE LOVERS

They come glowing to the gates of the city,
Armed with tenderness,
Resolute to parade
Beneath the windows of the cold women,
With their gifts warm on their shoulders.

The women sit frigidly smiling in their frames,
And their eyes are the eyes of Medusa.
Who but lovers,
Who but unslaked lovers may be starved so?

There is one bird left in the city of the cold women,
Forager of doorsteps,
Cosset of cold women.
It is sweet carrion they scatter to him.

VOICES

Are there words thin enough for such thin lips?
Smiles are more tenuous than laughter,
And their only echo is pain.

HOUSES

The roofs of the city are a bleak mist
Brooding over the sharpness beneath them:
Walls stroked to corners by the hands of the cold women,
Fireplaces for irony.
We shall not wonder at rimed mirrors –
Windows give up their secrets,
Not mirrors.

In the houses of the city of cold women
There are shadows.
They may be children,
They titillate the light so bashfully.

There are tired lilies, propped to apathy.

GARDENS

The white gardens of the cold women,
Sowed with crystal,
Budding in ivory –
They are like the cold women themselves.

They do not bend on their stalks.
They do not wilt.
How should they wilt?
They have no fragrance to repine in.

INTERLUDE

If ever, in the city of the cold women,
You should hear the stealthy fervor of a sound,
It is myself
Slinking furtively through silent streets,
Like a brave young spring
That comes gallantly to prove its warmness.

To an Unborn Child
Being New Intimations on Immortality

What! Another?

Once you were only the fragrance of a thought.
Now you will be a word forgotten in Babel.

Yet dream on and sweetly dream,
And doubly tranquil then,
For there is sorrow here for your bewilderment.

Dream the legend of man
From all that ever was
To all that is,
And be yourself the future.

(They say that, Proteus-like,
You make a pageant in the womb
As one might walk in sleep
And play his dreams.)

A wistful exhortation mine:
Crown not your sleep with wakefulness,
For life is drear fulfillment
Of an immortality of dreams.
Childhood is a humility.
Manhood is a regret,
And death is a repentance for having ever lived.

Oh little thing,
Heedless intention of your dreams,
Recoil and dream another dream
For shift of life.

Else will you mar the sweetness of eternity
With one brief moment of being.

Initiation

When the women of twelve summers
Of the tribe of Kee-haldo
Polish their backs in the sunlight
With the loam that lies on the left bank of the Teev
And put on the girdles of red seed and beetle rock
That they have been beading all year,
Then the Wise Man of the white sky
Tears another blue leaf off the tree
That will be bare some day
When the women of twelve summers
Of the tribe of Kee-haldo
No longer polish their backs in the sunlight.

Tareek! Tareek!
Zafoo the Wise Man of Kee-haldo,
Zafoo of the yellow wens
Has rounded his pit in the earth
Ten dances above the head of Bogil,
Who is the Old Man of Life and Death
That lives in the middle of the earth

And has no ears
And can't hear questions
And has no tongue
And can't answer them.

But Zafoo the Wise Man of Kee-haldo,
Zafoo sits in his rounded pit
And listens to the questions of the women of twelve summers
And dips the claw of a green tiger that the moon once killed
Into the venom of a blue-fanged snake
And writes his answers every year
On the polished backs of the women of twelve summers.

Tareek! Tareek!
The women of twelve summers cry out
When Zafoo carves his answers on their backs.
And they hide the pain behind their eyes
So that their husbands won't know what Zafoo said,
So that their children won't know what Zafoo said,
So that nobody will ever know,
Nobody but Bomidja the Carrier
Who takes women home to Bogil when they die.
Tareek! Tareek!
Listen to the women of twelve summers cry out
When Zafoo carves his answers on their back.

Listen to the girls of eleven summers
Laughing in the wet forest,
Picking red berries from white-leafed bushes,
Digging up beetle rocks with their toes
And counting on their fingers
The questions they'll ask
When their girdles are strung
And their backs polished
With the loam that lies on the left bank of the Teev.

Starved

Who owns this body of mine?
Not him to whom I gave it for a moment
To test the longing limit of his flesh upon,
Nor yet myself, its guardian.

Who owns this body of mine,
Come, take it back.
I have not fare enough for both of us.

Who owns this body of mine?
Will no one claim it?
I cannot bear to leave it so.
Pity me,
Pity the orphan frame,
Hungering together –
Death is the final crust
Of our poor provender.

Fallacies

I

He never would have been a man to feed
Her subtleties, saying: You're like a tree
In moonlight, when he meant that she
Was wrapped in her own shadows, and yet he
Succeeded obscurely in pleasing her
Because perhaps he had a smile that seemed
To understand ten times as much as he
Could ever see himself. She almost loved
Him for that smile, but with a troubled sense
Of its unfitness. For his eyes were like
Two empty cups whose substance had been poured
To fill a disappointment, and there was
No more of him than that – two empty eyes
That hung above his smile like two old pools
Too shallow for a young and slender moon

233

To rest upon. She'd warn him laughingly
And say that if he'd ever lose that smile
He'd lose her too, for she'd ride off on it
Up to the sky where it belonged. But he
Began to think she meant himself when she
Had only meant his smile, and came to love
Her in a giddy way that chased his smile,
For it had paradoxically been
A rare sophisticated little thing.
She waved him then a frivolous farewell.
Goodbye, she said, I'm going riding, Sir!

II

This one she likened to a dragon fly,
He came to poise on her so nervously
And hover in a dogged queasy way
Round her indifference as if he might
Delicately prick her inattention.
He did not want to play the butterfly,
Not that he was afraid of what she had
To give but rather that he was too fond
Of his despondency, having as lief
Be still the weeping flagellant upon
Her hand and worry his wan wings until
They titillated her desire, but she
Had heeded him as little as if he'd been
A wind. So having scorned her lips and found
Her hand insensible when he had come
To brood upon it tragically, he thought
In a soft melancholy mood, to mind
His lady of a horned asp that once
Had been allowed the gentle liberty
Of Cleopatra's bodice. But she laughed
At him unfeelingly and cried: "Poor thing,
You're too ambitious for a dragon fly!
How can you woo me when you have no sting?"
He made a brittle armor of his wings
And all his slenderness was changed into
A plump and middle-aged disconsolateness
While he crawled off with wounded memories
To trust his soul to a lugubrious beetle.

III

It would be an unpardonable cliché
To say that he danced to the tune she played
If he were not a man absurdly like
A dunder-pated circus bear that had
Been trained to a pathetic merriment
For his own imbecility, and he
Had hopped so long to her *pizzicatos*
That he began to feel that she was now
No longer his accompanist, but that
He had come to be hers, and so he went
Collecting pennies in the audience
For her like an organ-grinder's monkey.
Oh, she was never cruel to him, and yet
She was more savage in her gentleness
Than if she'd roundly beaten him, and sent
Him capering alone, for very soon
Her pretty beast began to witness how
She loved an untaught tiger better than
His tutored skill, and he said to himself:
"I will be fierce, oh fondly fierce, enough
To make her fear enough to fancy me,
And I will growl, oh sweetly growl, enough
To show how much I'd growl if it were not
Herself I was tenderly growling at."
He tugged his chain and gently growled at her,
Enough to make her laugh more tenderly
Than had his proudest tricks, and fondly laugh
Until he sadly ambled off. For how
Could Bruno growl again since she had laughed
At him, and how could Bruno dance again
Since he had learned just what it was to growl?

IV

She says her merchandise is images –
I might add something else, a little store
Of esoteric humor that is sold
To those alone who have the proper coin
(If there are any such) – and whispers then

As seriously as a worried child
That there's no profit in her trade because
She draws too much upon her stock herself,
Leaving the poorest choice to customers.
It was so she apologized to me
For her extravagance when she began
To speak of him. She told me that he was
Her prodigal and that the figures she
Had bought to deck each small return of his
In quaint festivity, would surely reach,
If bordered end to end, the echo of
The farthest cry some vagrant poet might fling
To call his doughtiest imagining.
But best of all she liked to say that he
Was like a patchwork shawl to wrap her in.
And she was not afraid that it might grow
Too thin for her, for each time that he came,
He lightly spoke some little brilliant thing
That could be stitched into her shawl, until,
She said, it was as pied as Joseph's coat –
Some smooth, anaemic word of Marivaux's,
A saucy cretonne of Voltaire's, or else
A gracious verse of Horace's all stitched
Together with some gay quips of his own
With corners so acutely trenchant that
They fitted as demurely in the others
As if the cloak were woven of one cloth.
So she rejoiced to think how she went dressed
In what he said, unwisely so, for he
Began to think it was himself she loved
And not his words, and fell to loving her
Himself. Then humor fled from him as once
Another's smile had fled before the fear
Of love's solemnity. His silence was
The worse to bear for all that he had spoken.
Her shawl grew threadbare and he never could
Be brought to patch it up again, while she
Went shivering through a silent season
And then dismissed him angrily, saying
She would not let herself be denuded
By anybody's taciturnity.

Improprieties

I

Your hands are very white.
What fierceness have they fingered
To grow so delicate, so pale?
Are your feet whiter yet
And still more timorously slender
That they step so obscurely?
Are you afraid of hurting me
That you do not go barefooted?
But I am more aggrieved that two white shames
Should patter virtuously in sandals,
Demurely shod.

II

Why do you come indecorously bearing
Clusters of lilacs faceted elegantly?
They are an immorality to your chasteness.
For you are stark and inornate
And your hair is smooth and unfragrant
And your eyes are cold chalcedony
And your lips are a thin sharpness
And all the rest of you a dear severity.

III

Why do you come fantastically folded
In a reticent dark gown?
It is the house of a harlot
And you are white and unclothed inside.
Do you think you can dwell there
Cryptically forever
And yet be wantonly unviolated?

But your gayest indecency
Is your garrulity
That lecherously enwraps your silence.
When will you be bared of your frivolity
And come to me mutely, modestly serious?

For One Who Will Dust a Shadow

Take out your speckled shadow
From its cupboard, in the morning.
Softly brush it,
Lest you crush it
And leave your body bare
With no shadow to wear.

And lift your little body
From its bed, in the morning.
When you've dressed it
And caressed it
In each careful counted way, then,
Put the speckled shadow on.

If at noon it may be found
Like a scarf upon your shoulder,
Be at dusk a little bolder,
Trail your shadow on the ground.

But at night, put away
Your shadow in its cupboard
That is empty all day
And upon its little bed
Lay your tired little body
Well washed and fed.

If you take these troubles
Exactly enough
To wear yourself out
In an accurate measure,
Then you and your body and your speckled shadow
Will all wear out quite evenly together
With nothing left over.

The Floorwalker

His ways were ribboned aisles –
    A beetle in a flower bed,
Brittle with polished smiles
    And stiff severity. (It's said
That ladies all require
Some firmness in a squire.)

His coat was very green
    And brushed to a thin dignity.
They say he was as lean
    As his worn affability.
And yet they loved him for
The gallantry he wore.

For his humility
    He knew this liberal redress:
That he might ever be
    A catalogue of loveliness:
"Silks, laces, kerchiefs or
Brocades on the third floor."

One night when all was done
    He died apologetically.
That night there was begun
    Another walking wistfully.
What fate could be more dire –
To be Nobody's squire?

Soon the last webs of riddled clay
Crumble, the essence leaks away.
Death gathers the decay.

And the disintegration bears the honored name
Of mind. The heart that drills receives the same
Homage of character. Man lays the blame

Of agony on death, pardons the pain,
Forgets how trees attain
Death intactly and unslain,

Since death is sense and sense the thrust
Of violation in the quiet crust
That guards the dust.

There is no mending. The habits of this wisdom break
The vessel and expose the dregs we make
Of the dark restless fluid we mistake

For wine to spill, but is the very blood
Of peace we should
Preserve each drop, to grow and wither like the green wood.

The Spring Has Many Silences

The spring has many sounds:
Roller skates grind the pavements to noisy dust.
Birds chop the still air into small melodies.
The wind forgets to be the weather for a time
And whispers old advice for summer.
The sea stretches itself
And gently creaks and cracks its bones....

The spring has many silences:
Buds are mysteriously unbound
With a discreet significance,
And buds say nothing.

There are things that even the wind will not betray.
Earth puts her finger to her lips
And muffles there her quiet, quick activity....

Do not wonder at me,
That I am hushed
This April night beside you.

The spring has many silences.

Napoleon in the Shades

The news! The news!
Find me in the news!
This I did, this I said,
What happened in Italy,
What happened in Egypt –
    Read for me, my eagle.

No word,
Forgotten.
Write in some journal of the dead
What I'll be doing to-day, to-morrow
And let the living read
In an old, out-of-date encyclopedia
What happened in Italy,
What happened in Egypt.
    Bird, the news!

The Circus

The trained men tumble hereditarily.
The ring master has lost his way
Back to the music, the band being
Not the same choir simple
Of primate tunes, as in the old days,
But a careful dissonance
Drowning elaborately the lost theme.

To fly the instant of the opening
Up to her lips and sing
Red ambergris into her eyes
Until a west unbleeds the skies
And she can keep
Gaze on no sun but sleep.

Be certain in any midnight storm
Streaking the moor, it is Mary's form
Flashing the nightmare and the man
Sullen in her more Christian.
For it's only through smiling and kissing on the moor
Mary can be pure.

The Only Daughter

Under her gown the girl is
And alone as any lonely daughter.
She is kept in green because
Green silk is nearly water

And removes her as she is nearly white.
Mother slept through her birth.
Father was with the coals that night
At a study of sparks by the hearth.

It was forgotten she came naked.
In the morning she was put in wool.
Her face left bare but blended
With the house out the window cool.

She has grown and has been given
Day by day unknown and dressed
The quiet mysteries of woman
Unwitting of the rhapsodist.

But it is dangerous to keep an only daughter
Like Atlantis or an isle
Sunken in green water
Through which may rise a smile.

She smiles and she is golden
About her mouth waving.
Her smile only will be stolen
And the mouth not worth saving

Will spread smooth and green
Over no more hunger.
How warm is chill if seen
When the body is yet younger

Than a green gown and the gown
Ripples like a summer winter
As the lotus-lilies drown
Of an only daughter.

The Contraband

The old feet will never find pavements in the sky.
The new-found wings cannot etherealize earth's solid dust.
Invention but confirms the natural habit
And man's miracles obstruct the perfect paradox.

Otherwise, faith, that is not mechanical,
Might be the New Destroyer,
Set sunshine upon the throne of thunder,
Teach the topsy-turvy feet to kick the earth away,
Doubt the pedestrian deduction
And believe in the promenades of air
In spite of all appearances.

Life, then, like feet may profit from this philosophy,
Discover the free will,
Count death not necessarily logical
But one choice out of many,
Lick death from under it, ungravitational...
Something will whirl in to tread upon
As long as legs and life know how
To love and brave freedom and faith under them.

So Christ conquered and calmed the sea.
This is not idle and a comedy.
If death takes the hands of all those sinking Peters,
It is no fault of Christ or any other successful immortal,
But of the fixed fright that will not walk the waters,
And of the faint foot glued to an adhering world.
The clinging is of the foot only.

I have no doubt
The theory of death can be thwarted by theory,
And the poetical proof is good enough for me
As it has been for all my ancestral arguers.
We settle this difficult subject satisfactorily,
Believe every word we sing,
Insist that eternity is not impossible
And, preoccupied with paradox,
Smuggle a little forbidden beauty into the pale of being...
And, who knows?
Perhaps it is the very magic that contrives the trick!

For One Who Will Love God

Life and love together came
To fill my double cup
And I learned a fatal game
For using my life up.

Love was still the infinite
It had been at my birth.
I'd no way of spending it
On any heart on earth;

Till my love found out the same
Invention of slow death
In another deadly game
Where God lives on love's breath.

Mater Invita

Take him away,
This child I bore to-day.
Let me not look upon his face.
Take him to some far, unremembering place.
I have to do with birth
But not with mothering. The earth,
That never learned her pain through him
Nor felt the thrust of his mysterious limb
Against her side, will be his guardian
And watch my child becoming man.
I love the wound, I cannot love the sword
That lunged itself beneath my flowering sward
Of being and discovered to myself this heart
Of anguish bleeding now under the weapon's dart.

Take him away, take him away.
Perhaps one other day,
When the new wound is healed,
I may be wandering in a fresh field
Of wheat and in a stranger's eyes,
Who too must love this good tan grass, there recognize
The common grudge of each of us.
Greeting would be superfluous.
I shall but smile and hope he's like enough to me
To pardon an old enemy.

For One Who Will Go Shivering

"The twenty sunny shawls you had,
Some striped, some tessellated,
You would not be so cold, so sad,
Had ruth on prudence waited."

"The shawls I had when I was born,
With fringe and foreign pattern,
One gave I to a wench forlorn,
Another to a slattern.

"I wish this mossy, flimsy stuff
Had been embroidered double:
The last one was not fine enough
To give a knave in trouble.

"So this I keep upon my shelf,
For I could never bear it
That one as shivering as myself
Should pass and see me wear it."

For One Who Will Stand in the Wind

Halt here a minute,
Winds, waters, scurrilous dust
Spitting my senses at me,
Contemptuous.

Stop long enough,
Make way enough.
Little the land and air I occupy.
Rivers run past such as I
Ungossiping to the sea
With no treasured drift of me.

Slight my space,
Short my minute,
Commensurate with what I am.
Yet scorn me disproportionately,
Not at all, comrades,
Since out of nearly nothing
I cry a brief equality
Who am small and great as this
Irrelevant antithesis.

Ode to Love

I

Oh, more than nothing and surely less than all
        And so ungodly we
        Our gods must go
Immortally under the coronal
        Of mere mortality, –
        We crawl too low
For your encounter, Love, yet you have lit
Prayer in our hearts that you might answer it;
And mercifully filled for us the flask
Of mercy you had bidden us to ask.
Who has not wet his lips and warmed his breast
With your wine's gush of fire and fountained kiss,
Nor felt the matin tap upon his crest
Of your enfingered dawn in this abyss,
Must stumble unenviable and unblest,
Nor envying our exaltation's bliss
        Who ride the flying field
        By Love revealed.

II

But an endearing envy is the spell
        Exasperating of
        Each maid and man
Who loves the other's lovelier lot so well
        That jealousy, for Love,
        Turns guardian.
Peace lies between, a laughing rivulet
That crossed in spite not love would quick bewet
The grudging heart with tears, dissolve the hate.
For passion makes the heart compassionate.
We that were frightening when loveless, small
To one another, Love has lessoned brave
And lifted to unterrifying tall,
Taught that Love's grief can prostrate but the slave,
Betrayal but the faithless can befall,
And those alone give Love an earthly grave

Who cannot climb above
To live with Love.

III

There are as many lusts demoniac
      As men that have no fate
      Beyond the flesh;
And life denies itself in those who lack
      Love's single adequate
      Of soul that fresh
In each new love dawns the discovery
Of joy and smiles the body's irony
On an immortal triumph sealed in soul
But broken bodily and yet left whole.
Lady of promises we need not keep
If we love true enough to pledge, forgive
Our forfeiture, since love broods like a sleep
Around the body that must wake to live
A life that floats the unremembered deep
Of convenanted dreams incarnative
      Out of the flesh and bone
      In sleep alone.

IV

Who was an Asiatic deity
      And deigned to blush beneath
      A Grecian sun,
Many a mediaeval love did she
      Grace like leaves that wreathe
      A modern one.
None need be knave that has a heart to sing
Love's praises, who can make each subject king.
Love will deny no warrior his pelf
Who winds no kingdom but denies himself.
If the lamenting lover on the stair
Of Love's steep throne mistake her tears for frown
Or find her too vertiginously fair,
Love will arise and soon come smiling down

The long escarpment of his shy despair
And humbly heal his fright and set her crown
        Upon him, in his stead
        To be upled.

                    V

Love, bide with us who pay our death too dear
        With love, till we lose death
        To you again.
Be then the living angel of our bier,
        Rescuer of the breath
        That cried its pain
The last of life, since pain came crying first.
But pain is still now and the body's worst
Of death is done. Release the body's best.
Let fly the voice that wept in bond to grief,
Now grief is gone, now singing soaringly
In thrall to Love, joy is the only fief
Of its deliverance. The voice is free,
The bird awaits the final frozen leaf,
Then breaks the snow grave of the bony tree,
        Flies from the wintery mouth
        To Love's still south.

        Poems to Alastor

        Prothalamion

Nothing alone, together whole,
Two lives apart cancel in death.
Two added lives will beat one breath.
Of time for an eternal soul.

With beauty tamed between us here
And each the other's lovely knowing
Of final space, we can be going
Singly around the mystic sphere

Of love; we can be coming back
To where we started, to die as two.
And I who bore the close of you
Can surely bear the lonely lack

That death shall make the mortal past
To the long present that fulfills
A faith for which our Hymen kills
The flesh to keep the spirit fast.

Prothalamion II

Where the beholding self of me is wrecked
In you and the world rattles to a death
Not noiseless but outcried in the quick breath
Of my renunciation, I reject

New lives of sound and vision and above
My spurned ghost fly an angel that died for you
To gain a lasting heaven of us through
The single sense of an exclusive love.

But I have risen to a lonely place,
Too worshipful in this immortal birth
To die again for a forbidden earth
That hides you like an absent god whose face
I have no sight but a blind love to see,
Groping along a lost eternity.

Instead

Instead, I have resumed the old discard
Of what I was and rememorialized
The interrupted minute I despised
For a forever where it was not hard
To be discovered and familiarized
By the fixed Orient of love that prized
A charted faith it knew not how to guard.

What sun is still enough always to lie
Horizoned holy in the changeless east?
See how the minute your impatience sped
Once more toward time is mended here and I
Drift back into a life that brings, at least,
A promised death you should have brought instead.

Beauty Was Once...

Beauty was once, Alastor, where you left
Upon my lips or lighted in my eyes
A longing that assumed this fair disguise
That it might be endured and I not reft
Of grace the eve of passion and the theft
Was pardonable since I would surprise
A destined loveliness with one that dies
To greet it when the patient night is cleft.

Why have you never come and brought the dawn?
The false, dark bloom of my expectancy
Went trustfully, made way for the true flower
You failed to ask of me, freeing the pawn
Before it had redeemed my love for me
From the marred sorrow of this barren hour.

The Bridge

Love lies Alastor like a broken bridge
Between us as the world dissolves and leers
Impassable and watery. My tears befog,
Befog us both and hide the rescued ridge
Of hope from which I meant me to be seen
Watching, if you should look toward me again
Remembering who gave you sight and fain
To be forgiven. Grief bleeds my heart serene
And still. The waters widening run red.
My body breaks under the sin of pride
That dared to think love might, perhaps, reside
In it. Swift and forever I am dead
And clear of mist, with wings I must implore
To flight, though now we prowl on the same shore.

Ghosts

Alastor, if I may swoon to you and you a sun
Stark over my withering,
Earth may claim carefully the dust dethroned
And fill her treasury again.

Only take the crown that soars, twirls toward you
As death dwindles and burns,
And pause before the faithlessness to think
That each new birth of love ennobled under it
Will bear my spiteful memory repeatedly.

This Side

Oh now, Alastor, I am well divided.
That side I am not,
This side I am, am a whole half,
Since the half you have of me is a choked intruder,
Crushed to a pain-pulp.

Love has combed away the wonder.
Very prim, very plain is my established day.
Dreams sharpen the border,
But to what use yonder?
There is nothing for me far away,
There is a little for me here.

And easily as sleeping
I have left off weeping.
It is good where I am.
Grief is a trespass
That would lose me to you over.

There is nothing for me far away,
There is a little for me here.

Numbers

Being an upward thousand, man,
To your reiterated thin three,
An implicit passion and inevitable
To your thrice helpless poetry,
I can, after your counting and intoning of me,
Begin with flying four,
Forgetting how your calculation quailed,
As was my valedictory mercy able
To baptize you Alastor
And take at least your name along
Since I could never invoke you as you were.

Nor do I scorn the feeble measures you hummed
Of my progressive song,
Nor do I claim you have not somehow summed
Your own full music if not mine.

The wonder is that over over,
One-two-three and one-two-three
Waltzes every bar of me,
Keeping time for upward thousand,
Haunting the vain way I have
Of newly numbering old love.

Plaint Not Bitter

Love sent Alastor to call my soul.
Wings only had my soul.
But oh! my body would go along with it,
My body that had but feet.

This way the wings folded and the body bore the soul.
This way I came too late
And found Alastor gone.

The single pain upon the feet,
The single pain upon the wings,
The double pain within my heart –
These are no blame of his or mine,
But of a soul with wings that cannot walk,
But of a body without flying feet.

261

The Fourth Wall

A man was on each wall of three.
He passed his prime, each one, and went,
Was over, as men are, and free
For trouble elsewhere, when the walls fell.
But not so she, not she, not she.
Women do not pass so easily.
And though she rotted, rumbled first,
And though her stones trembled the worst,
She last of all allowed cement,
Where she had been, to let in hell.

Her father, husband and her son
Stood back and body to their place,
But like her mother, she was one
Of Deborah's daughters, her battle was
In the vale to voice high Lebanon,
To muster strong, while men were gone,
The hosts of shelter and to house,
Smiling, a spirit and a mouse
Guarding eyes up and open the face
Of home each man in keeping has.

So she was longer to fall down brave,
Stood thinking in a habit of
Doors open hearty though the grave
Was closed three times about her, square;
Stood between air and like a stave
Of death defied her earth to save
One windfall of her as a wall
Still leaning on heaven though no more tall
Than any old head brought down by love
To kiss the dust that shares its care.

Song of the Lyre

Laughter in love changes every age
As light changes. The sun is never the same.
But the night of love is old.
It is still the lyre that strikes the hour
That scarce can reach for sorrow
Out of the shadow.

The strings will be seven to the days always.
The music of our fingers in the dark
Is frantic, is the rain of blind moths
Out of the false heaven
Day but to flee, day but to give night.
O it is mercy we are women,
We can lie to the earth low
As if for sin, though sinned against,
And listen. The lyre is buried but it plays.
We may fold our fingers
And more humble be.
Not Orpheus has the lyre
But Eurydice.

Free

Thinking is the poorest way of traveling –
       Paths in the head,
       Dreams in bed.

Living in a body is the drearest kind of life,
       Locked up all alone
       In flesh and bone.

       Turn me out of head,
       Turn me out of body,
       Wake me out of bed.

Rather than respectable,
Vagabond and dead.

My Hunger

My hunger has no crumbs but moments.
I am time.
I knew this yesterday, Alastor,
When your departure and my abdication
Struck identical.

My life devours me then, quietly.
Not too ravenously, quickly,
To discountenance the peace,
The full content of death.
Love only can abstain and starve not
Of the divine disquiet endless.
But going you gave me lovelessness and longing
And the accursed courage for a close.

For One Who Will Keep a Mirror

Beware a loveliness too smiling.
Laughter wrinkles,
Weeping wrinkles.
A face unfelled is calm's inadequacy.
Fury only fills the ruin assigned.

Smiles are but dreams of beauty.
Passions are first true then fair.
Therefore demand,
After the nightless intervention of your youth,
A darker season of humor,
Pitched on a beach of shells
Split visible to tides again
Over your face where the deep violence of scars
Prolongs in still flesh
Inbred in the immortal bone
The blessed signs that will outlast
The passing pleasantry,
Even the more abiding voice.

Three Miles Away

Three miles away lay
The dusty truth among the weeds
Where it rolled like a loose ball
And toppled still and tired.

Wind and rain
Wore it clean.
It could be seen,
White and lovelier
Than any washed flower,
Three miles away
Where it licked and cuddled lay.

But three miles away
Are an enemy.
Many tramped half a rod,
Many tramped a whole.
Many steady travelers
Dreamed a mile toward the goal.
But supper steamed at home
And sang a spice
Into cowardice.
The trickling torment of the tongue,
When an obscurer lust is stung
With the uncertain white
Of a more indefinable delight,
Wins over three miles,
Steams up a mist,
Blinds back the eyes
Toward the more answerable appetite
That may permit paradise
Tempting among the weeds
After the closer needs
Of evening and the night
Are tended and the day
Slips off like sleep
To three miles away.

For One Who Will Sing

Bind you to the back of a bird.
Be strong-lifted.
Follow the wind,
Listening, answering,
Giving songs for song.

Still on your cross,
Arms stretched to wing,
Let one say
It is you who sing.
Let none tell
How silent a bird may be.

But measure your flight,
Wing upon wing.
Lash little songs upon your throat
In a clear agony
Till it is mute and broken enough.

Unbind you, then
From the back of a bird.
Drift swiftly,
Drop soundlessly
Into the sea,
Letting all know at last
How silent a bird may be.

For One Who Will Believe

It is!
And all is all you see.
You must never turn the leaf over,
You must never hew the tree.
Faith is the modesty of self-approval.

It was.
The preference of certainty is past.
But the assured season will take confidence,
Return a rose as lovely as the last,
Find in the new retinue
A faint pride reminiscent of you.

How I Called the Ant Darling

The moment must have been the same for both.
For, as my foot went down to kill it,
Darling, Darling, screamed it,
And Darling, Darling, I answered it,

Lifting on the crackling pieces,
And once more Darling as once more down.
Then it did not cry or turn.
My mouth stopped tasting Ant.

Death-making lost disgust,
Or death went from both, and it was
Darling, Darling, with no thought of pardon,
As if the dead and death-maker clasped hands,

Watching the thing.
So it was Darling, Darling,
Yet no peace, for I ached
As much as like Ant I could feel,

Not much: I could not crawl
Or break up so small.
My leg thought pain, but was too high
To see, except the humane toes

Drew in to hug the deed.
So Darling, in my mouth
Wore the sharp slaughter off.

The next breath, too, said Darling, but looking up
From murder with no purer word,
I breathed it no less tender
Not for an Ant and not for murder.

Appendices

Appendix A

Bibliographical notes to Sequence V

'Dimensions', *The Fugitive*, 2, August-September 1923, p.124.
'A Pair', *Nomad*, 2, Autumn 1923, p.9.
'Adjustment', *The Lyric West*, 3, November 1923, p.5.
'The Lightning', *The Step Ladder*, 8, December 1923, p.3.
'The City of Cold Women', *Poetry*, 23, January 1924, pp.188-90.
'To an Unborn Child', *The Fugitive*, 3, February 1924, p.9.
'Initiation', *The Fugitive*, 3, February 1924, pp.12-13.
'Starved', *The Fugitive*, 3, February 1924, p.14.
'Fallacies', *Poet Lore*, 35, Spring 1924, pp.153-156.
'Improprieties', *The Fugitive*, 3, April 1924, pp.56-57.
'For One Who Will Dust a Shadow', *The Fugitive*, 3, April 1924, p.58.
'The Floorwalker', *Contemporary Verse*, 17, June 1924, p.91.
'To the Sky', *Contemporary Verse*, 17, p.92.
'For One Who Will Bless the Devil', *The Fugitive*, 3, August 1924,
     p.124.
'A Consolation', *The Lyric*, 4, September 1924, p.8.
'Across a Hedge', *Sewanee Review*, 32, October 1924, p.1.
'Forms', *The Fugitive*, 3, December 1924, p.143.
'Wanderer', *Sewanee Review*, 33, January 1925, p.56.
'To a Broken Statue', *The Lyric*, 5, February 1925, p.4.
'For One Who Will Remember', *The Lyric*, 5, March 1925, p.2.
'Summary for Alastor', *The Fugitive*, 4, March 1925, p.7.
'The Higher Order', *The Fugitive*, 4, March 1925, p.10.
'The Spring Has Many Silences', *The Lyric*, 5, April 1925, p.12.
'Napoleon in the Shades', *Voices*, 4, May-June 1925, p.215.
'The Circus', *The Fugitive*, 4, June 1925, pp.52-53.
'Mary Carey', *The Fugitive*, 4, September 1925, pp.71-72.
'The Only Daughter', *The Fugitive*, 4, September 1925, p.73.
'The Contraband', *The Calendar of Modern Letters*, 2, October 1925,
     pp.92-3.
'For One Who Will Love God', *Contemporary Verse*, 20, September
     1925, p.41.
'Mater Invita', *Contemporary Verse*, 20, September 1925, p.41.
'For One Who Will Go Shivering', *Literary Review of the New York
     Evening Post*, October 10, 1925, p.3.
'For One Who Will Stand In the Wind', *Voices*, 5, October 1925, p.11.

271

'Ode to Love', *The Reviewer*, 5, October 1925, pp.17-19.

'Poems to Alastor', *Voices*, 5, December 1925, pp.92-97.

'The Fourth Wall', *The Fugitive*, 4, December 1925, p.109.

'Song of the Lyre', *The Lyric*, 5, December 1925, p.4.

'Free', *The Nation* (New York), 122, January 27, 1926, p.89.

'My Hunger', *Palms*, 3, January 1926, p.105.

'For One Who Will Keep a Mirror', *Palms*, 3, January 1926, p.106.

'Three Miles Away', *Palms*, 3, January 1926, p.107.

'For One Who Will Sing', *Palms*, 3, March 1926, p.179.

'For One Who Will Believe', *The Nation* (New York), 123, August 11, 1926, p.130.

'How I Called the Ant Darling', *Two Worlds*, 2, December 1926, p.114.

Appendix B

The following poems have been moved to Sequence V for the reason stated in the editorial note:

From Sequence I: The Fourth Wall, Improprieties.
From Sequence II: A Pair, The Spring Has Many Silences,
                   Starved, To An Unborn Child, The City of
                   Cold Women.
From Sequence III: Across a Hedge, Adjustment, To a Broken
                   Statue, A Consolation, Fallacies, The
                   Floorwalker, The Lightning, Mary Carey,
                   The Only Daughter, Song of the Lyre.

The following poems have been omitted since they already appear in some form in the *Collected Poems* of 1938 or in one of the nine volumes on which that book drew:

From Sequence II: The Tillaquils.
From Sequence III: All Right, And the Pain, Because I Sit Here
                   So, Chronicle Chapters, Chrysalid, Daniel,
                   Elegy (For Amalthea), Many Gentlemen,
                   Nothing, One Right One Left,
                   Philosopher's Morrow, Sonnets in Memory
                   of Samuel, Take Hands.
From Sequence IV: Lucrece and Nara, Materials in the
                   Mysteries, No More Are Lovely Palaces,
                   Back to the Mother Breast, Any Cat.
From Sequence V: The Quids, Mortal, Lying Spying, The Sad
                   Boy, Druida, Virgin of the Hills, As from a
                   Balcony (from Poems to Alastor).

One other poem from Sequence V, Saturday Night (published first in *The Fugitive*, 3, December 1924) has been omitted since it was included in an appendix to the Carcanet Press edition of the *Collected Poems* (1980).

Appendix C

The year 1925, during which Laura Riding Gottschalk selected and rejected poems for her first collection, *The Close Chaplet* (1926) (see Editors' Introduction, p.xiii), also saw the appearance of her first published essay on poetry: it has not been reprinted until now, and has received little critical attention. 'A Prophecy or a Plea' appeared in *The Reviewer*, 5(2), April 1925, pp.1-7; in the following text a few misprints and small matters of punctuation have been silently corrected. The quotation from Francis Thompson is from the beginning of his poem, 'Of Nature: Laud and Plaint'. No source has been identified for the Italian phrase parenthetically applied to Francis Thompson.

With this essay, the Editors have decided to publish a stray early poem, 'Address to Shelley', found in typescript carbon among the James M. Frank papers in the Fugitive collection at Vanderbilt University.

Address to Shelley

Shelley, that I love you well
Is in no wise a reason I should vow
To be late advocate
Of the last fretful century's bestirrings:
Surely yourself would not be Shelley now?

If I feed better on your form
Than on your faith, it is, we need not zeal
These times. We are persuaded.
We are as wild with love of truth, to build
Her body and proclaim the passion real.

Of your fierce suit and argument
And dauntless wooing, I may fairly reap,
Since you were awed and shy
Of the embrace, and more inspired to love
A dream than to possess a broken sleep.

But in this wakefulness what bride
Awaits me? Is she bright as mine or pale
As yours would be of longing?
How can I claim more modernly than you
The changing countenance behind the veil?

274

A Prophecy or a Plea

The most moving and at once distressing event in the life of a human being is his discovery that he is alive. From that moment to his death the fact of life is a constant white glare over him, an unsetting and shadowless sun. For darkness, for repose, for a quiet examination of the conditions of existence, for the experience of appreciation and pleasure, it is found necessary to close the eyes, to create an interior where life is a dim infiltration through the heavy curtains of the flesh into this dark room of the soul and where, so seen, through eyes reopened in a more endurable light, it appears lovely, describable. Art has become an evocation of the shadows.

What has happened? We have been blinded by life, so we turn our senses inward, against it; and the utterance of relief is made in pride, the cry of cowardice becomes the authentic act of art. The tradition of art, of poetry especially, as a catharsis has so thoroughly legitimized this process that it is almost impossible to attack it. It is not a question of proving another method more legitimate. There is no other method. For if the matter be examined more closely it will be seen that the quarrel must be made not with the way we write but with the way we live. For art is the way we live, while aesthetics, in divorcing art from life, sets the seal of approval upon the philosophy of escape. We live life by avoiding it. Art then as the strategy of this philosophy is no more than an inversion, and, as an inversion, is barren. It is not, as it should be, the conduct of life itself, but merely an abnormality of conduct.

Life, then, may be an experience in which we are the passive objects of a force to which our nature offers no resistance, but transmits the shock of impact to the functions of poetry. In this definition man is but a stream of passage between the source that is life and the outlet that is poetry. The climate of this stream, its slight waves and winds and temporary havens constitute the notion of beauty. The artist of this mood sees it not as an inexhaustible infinity of the source whose entirety he is able to reconstruct from his partial vision of it or as the ultimate mold of the mysterious vessel into which life flows. The quality of beauty is rather an accidental, a peculiar flavor of the poet's own soul, an isolated phenomenon, the taste of a wine rather than the very pulse of running blood. The taste may be whatever pleases the whim of the moment. There is no eternal form, no ideal. Something vague

275

as a flood pours in upon the being, something in excess of it that becomes unbearable until poetry or another muse, like an old phlebotomist, performs the operation that lets the magic or the accursed fluid out. It is this attitude toward life that has inspired almost every poet who has suffered or rejoiced in living and cried out in art. To the poet of classical tradition art is the measure of self-control against the violence of existence. To the old romanticist (I mean to speak of another) it is the flourish of escape from one impossible world into another. Does the modern realist do better? The test of his art is the quantity of life compressed in his work. The expressionist lives in a realm that is neither art nor life but a limbo that borrows from both and belongs to neither. The impressionist achieves an unhappy blur of art and life in which he himself is obscured. But the differences between all these lie in no fundamental quarrel of values but in personal eccentricities of method. For all the rôle of art is medicinal. For the poets of the classical mold it is a strong cathartic that keeps them free of malaise and dyspepsia and wraps them in an urbane Horatian peace; for the Elizabethan, a pretty pastoral constitutional; for all the romantics, a drug – a stimulant for Byron, a delicious dose of laudanum for Shelley (even such as Baudelaire bought their cocaine at the same shop); a soothing syrup for the Victorians; a tonic for the realists; a heady wine for the impressionists; a profound emetic for the expressionists. In this strange company – the earnest Theocritus, the author of the unhappy and magical *Pervigilium Veneris*, the divine Dante, the seraphic Keats, the slobbering Swinburne, even the modern female lyricists who squeal with dainty passion under the fine pin-pricks of life – the poetic tradition accomplishes the vitiation of life in art. The pressure of life is unbearable and the poet in this hazard does not hurl himself against it but finds a safety-valve in song; and existence, that art should have spiritualized, becomes despiritualized in art.

Now I am insisting that the pressure is a challenge not to a retreat into the penumbra of introspection but to the birth of a new poetic bravery that shall exchange insight for outsight and envisage life not as an influence upon the soul but the soul as an influence upon life. The age of creation that was initiated by the Renaissance extends to-day to the physical aspects of life alone. For the rest we might as well be living in the Middle Ages. Our minds, compared to the noisy world inhabited by the flesh, are recesses of cathedral quiet. Living is the inspiration, art is the expiration. As such it is critical rather than creative, a criticism of life rather than a recreation of it. Even so radical a poet as T.S. Eliot becomes, as a critic, thoughtfully traditional. Of two artists, he says, the one who is the better critic is likely to be the better artist. In other words, life takes precedence over art which is, as of old, the recollection in tranquility. But it is now life itself that discredits the order by leaving art so far behind that both have become meaningless. Mechanics outrun metaphysics. Do not Philistines lead the race? Do they say to the poets: 'You have lagged behind, lost contact with life, grown irrelevant and obscure'? The difficulty is to be settled not by trying to write poetry that the Philistines can understand but by outdistancing them in the very race they have set. For while poets have been the parasites of the spiritual world they were born to, sucking up old essences, these others have suffused the physical world with the breath of creation, they have turned visions into actualities. The artist too must turn producer: and his visions must be begotten not of the darkness that lies behind closed eyes but in the steady light of a life he not only confronts but, because he enters upon it fortified by personal faith alone, even creates. He will not recollect life, so that his art would seem touched with the past, but life will proceed from him as from a champion. He will be something of the warrior, something of the prophet. Shelley indeed had this sense of initiation, but Shelley's romanticism has the quality of departure, it escapes with its victories to hypothetical heavens and so is ineffectual on earth. Francis Thompson had it better than he, with a clearer sight, a more happily crystalized faith. In his own terms he certainly succeeded, certainly realized life through art, made his soul the agent of perfection in an imperfect life:

> Lo, here stand I and Nature, gaze to gaze,
> And I the greater!

The source of his faith we need not accept or reject. The real source was Francis Thompson. It does not matter what the source of Francis Thompson was. We need only see the identity of faith and the spirit of his art in him as a first cause from which life followed as an emanation, in Francis Thompson almost as a radiation, to which he gave meaning, truth, and, because his vision was complete, an organic beauty. Other more modern poets will be moved by other truths, other ideals. Perhaps the differences will be even more than nominal. But if they are to succeed, their constitution must contain some of the elements that went to make up Francis Thompson – the magic at the start (*non murato, ma veramente nato*), the power of wonder that begets wonder, and miracle, and prophecy. They will be egoists and romanticists all, but romantics with the courage of realism: they will put their hands upon the mysterious contour of life not to force meaning out of it, since unrelated to them it must be essentially meaningless to them, but press meaning upon it, outstare the stony countenance of it, make it flush with their own colors. It is impossible to foretell who the gods of this vigorous idealism are going to be. Probably, because these are going to be intensely human times, there will be no gods, but men and women possessed of a passion they can communicate to life. There will be not only a new romanticism but, because faith grows more personal, a new romance. There will be lovers, a little less worldliness, perhaps, and, if we can believe in one another – and what else will there be left to believe in by then? – love. There will be fewer poems written, less of "art", more of artists. The poet will cease talking in sophisticated half-tones to himself not so much because his oracles have become less esoteric as that men and women shall come to understand through the little poetry in them that without him life would be without significance. If he has been obscure in the past, if his art has had no bearing on life, the fault is not entirely his own. If he shrank from life it was because life could be a weapon in the hands of other human beings less sensitive than he and repulse him by its brutality into the fortresses of contemplation. It is the part of the plain man, then, to call upon his portion of idealism to convert the world into a more accessible place, kindlier, less terrible. There must be poets of peace, poets of politics before the poet proper can be seen not as a troubadour but as a teacher. In the meantime a few brave singers will go on singing *quand même*.

And they will sing more largely as they proceed, more naïvely as they conquer complexities by admitting them with simplicity. They will have the souls of children and the sense of men. Whitman more than any other was one of these. There do not seem to be others in these times. Foreign poets are either grotesquely up-to-date or out-of-date; they lack that final timeliness, that quality of self-possession that inspires at least the better English and American poets. But these nevertheless are still worshipping that old god, Experience: it is all there somewhere in life, the truth, you must only let life flow over you, inundate you, and it will leave behind with you the fine sediment of proper feeling. Here is the apotheosis of inertia. You are clay, life is a potter, it is very wonderful. A body of poetry is inspired, thrilling, lyrical, sentimental, cynical and helpless all of it, the poetry of effect. But who has ever learned anything from experience? We get nothing from it, we give everything to it. Development comes through self-exercise, not through being hammered upon. To these poets, however, life is looked upon as an absolute wealth into which one has only to plunge one's thumb to pull out a plum, not as a pudding we must not only make but even gather plums for. So Sandburg does not possess life, life possesses him, croons to him as to a child. The English poets, perfect and polite, are still busy saying the right thing. Even Masefield is mastered by his sea, he does not master it. Housman cries 'Love!' and 'Death!' from quiet English pastures. Edna St Vincent Millay echoes prettily 'Love!' and 'Death!' across the Atlantic. The New Englanders talk and talk wisely. T.S. Eliot and his imitators endeavor to show how their chastity and ennui remain intact through all their orgies of intellectual debauchery. But to all of these life is an unquestionable first premise of which all their wisdom is a deduction.

But the function of the poet, of the poetic mind, is inductive rather than deductive. Life needs proving in poetry as well as in science. Philosophy is but a compromise between fact and fancy. The poet of a new spiritual activity admits neither. He, the human impulse, is the only premise. He is the potter. He is the maker of beauty, since all form originates in him, and of meaning, since he names the content. Life is create with him. The poetry of this mood will have still the wonder, still the exaltation. But the wonder will proceed not from the accidental contacts with a life that comes to us as a visitation but from a sense of self that adventures so steadfastly, so awarely beyond it that its discoveries have the character of creation and the eternal element of self-destiny. Confronted by a terrifying, absorbing, fascinating universe, it does not cry out: 'How big, how terrifying, how fascinating!' and permit itself to be overcome by it, but answers it, since this universe, a thing apart, can be answered in no other way, atom for atom in a recreated universe of its own, a universe defiantly intelligible. For this poetry, song is not surrender but salvation. If the music will at first seem harsher than older tunes, it is because the new poet must be endowed with the ruthlessness of a pioneer. He is a little harder, a little more muscular because he is called upon to be equipped not merely for static ecstacy or despair but for a progress into an unexplored terrain. He will be rude as a violator because he must advance alone, gentle as a guide, because he must get others to follow him. His poetry may be less pleasant than that which came before it, but it will at any rate be more honest since he must prove it workable at least for himself. It may be more difficult because more metaphysical since he is preoccupied chiefly with meaning, but a meaning inevitably rhythmical and poetical since it is a barren life reborn, touched and shaded with accent, inflamed with his own soul and molded into a temporary or an eternal form that is a symbol of peace and reconciliation between the inner nature of a man and the external world without him.

There will not be many who will be able to go the whole way, to complete the entire cycle that identifies at its close the ideational world of man, that begins with him, with the presumably impersonal world, that ends with him. If it will be argued that the poets who travel only a portion of the way sing as well and more sensibly than those who go beyond, since they are less likely to lose themselves in philosophical pitfalls, that a cheerful poet clears a little road just long enough for rambling but not long enough to lead him astray, and that the way of analysis is the way of destruction, I can only answer that if one is faithful enough, constant enough, the analysis will induce the synthesis, the poet will come home: and he will have tramped the whole road, he will have seen. By taking the universe apart he will have reintegrated it with his own vitality; and it is this reintegrated universe that will in turn possess him and give him rest. If this voyage reveals a futility, it is a futility worth facing.